golf
NORTHERN IRELAND
a visitor's guide to golf on the Causeway Coast.

WELCOME

'HOME OF THE CHAMPIONS'

Editor:
Arnaldo Morelli

Art Editor:
Stephen Duke
Graphic design:
www.id-designs.co.uk

Staff Writers:
Arnaldo Morelli
Contributors: Brian Keogh, Paul Kelly, Kevin Markham, Daniela Morelli, Jeff Whyte, Christine 'Teeny' Dixon

Photographers:
Aidan Bradley, Kevin Murray, Michael Robinson
Advertising Team:
Daniela Morelli, Adrian Kerr, Clare Willis
Thanks: The publisher would like to thank the following for their assistance in compiling this guide:
Raymond Eakin, Aiden Bradley, Kevin Markham, Paul Kelly, Daniela Morelli, Jeff Whyte, Christine Dixon, Wayne Telford, Paul Cutler, Clare Willis, Deric Henderson, Willy Gregg, Alan Simpson, Sean Millar, Wilma Erskine, Michael McCrudden, Adrian McNeice, Michael Moss, Alan Hunter, Mark Steen, Thomas Johnston, Trevor Peacock, Noelle Boyle, Damien McEvoy, Jim Gillen, Ian Blair, Terry Kelly, Don Brockerton, Shaun Devenny, Terrance McFall, Clarke Duddy, David Jones, Sean McLaughlin, Vincent Agnew, Bob Cockcroft, Noelle Hyland & all the businesses who placed adverts, without them we wouldn't have been able to proceed.

A special thank-you goes to Mike Nesbitt 'MLA' whose interview on BBC Radio Ulster's Talkback programme in January 2012 inspired the idea for Golf Coast Northern Ireland.

Publisher:
Vanity Publications
Unit 27, Sperrin Business Park,
Ballycastle Road,
Coleraine.
Northern Ireland,
BT52 2DH
www.vanity-publications.com
info@vanity-publications.com
Tel: 0044 (0)28 7034 3283
Fax: 0044 (0)28 7035 7055

Printed: in Northern Ireland by WG Baird

Liability:
While every care was taken preparing this book the publishers cannot be held responsible for the accuracy of the information or any consequence arising from it. All course info is based on information supplied by the Clubs at the time of publication. We take no responsibility for the content of external websites whose addresses are published in this book.

Permissions:
Material may not be reproduced in any form without the written consent of the publisher. Please address such requests to Arnaldo Morelli at Vanity Publications.

© **Vanity Publications** 2012.

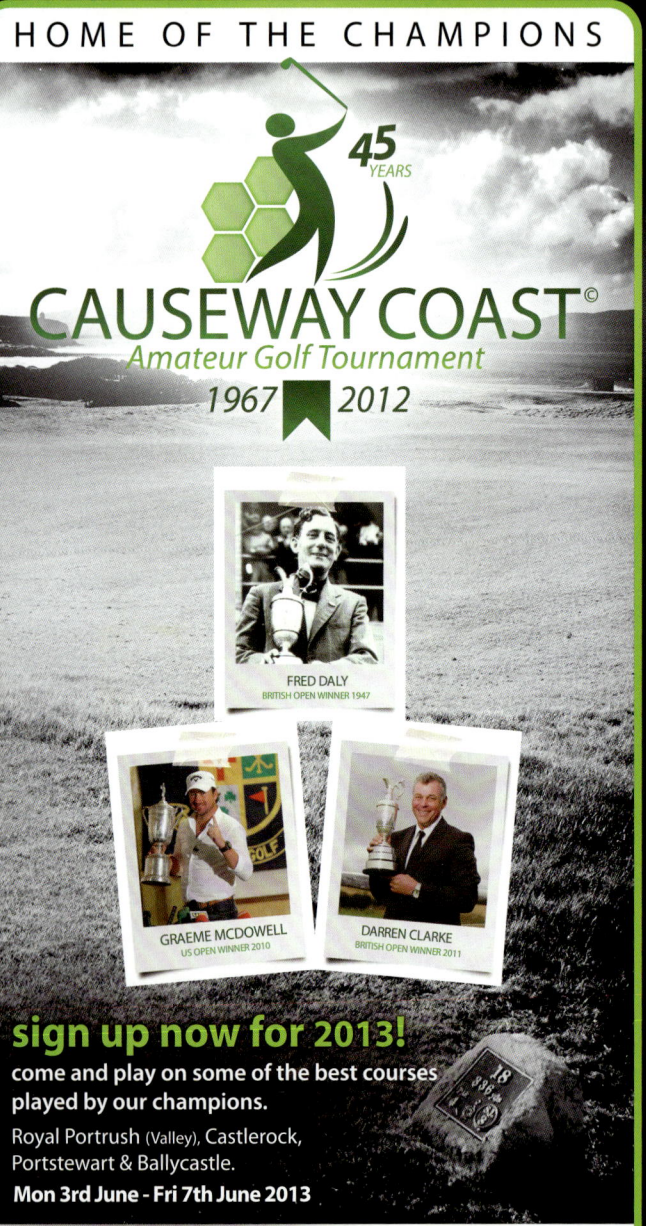

CONTENTS

Map & useful info	6-8
Introduction	**9-12**
Royal Portrush 'The Holy Grail'	13-20
New Kids on the tee	21&24
Local Heroes	25-31
The Irish Open returns	32-34
The Bushmills Dunes project	35-36
Course icon key	**38**
The Courses	**39-129**
Royal Portrush	40-58
Portstewart	60-72
Castlerock	74-85
Ballycastle	86-99
Gracehill	100-107
Roe Park	108-115
Bushfoot	116-121
Cushendall	122-126
Ballyreagh, Benone, Brown Trout	128-129
The Nineteenth Tourist Guide	**131**
Portrush	132-133
Ask yer Man! Willie Gregg	134-135
Portstewart	138-139
Coleraine	142-143
Downhill & Mussenden Temple	147
Ask yer Man! Alan Simpson	148-149
The Giants Causeway	150-151
Dunluce Castle	153
Bushmills	154-155
Carrick-a-Rede rope bridge	156
Ballycastle	160-161
The Causeway Coastal Route	159
Cushendall & The Glens of Antrim	162-163

The Courses

1. Benone
2. Castlerock
3. Portstewart
4. Ballyreagh
5. Royal Portrush
6. Bushfoot
7. Ballycastle
8. Cushendall
9. Gracehill
10. Brown Trout
11. Roe Park

golf coast
NORTHERN IRELAND
a visitor's guide to golf on the Causeway Coast.

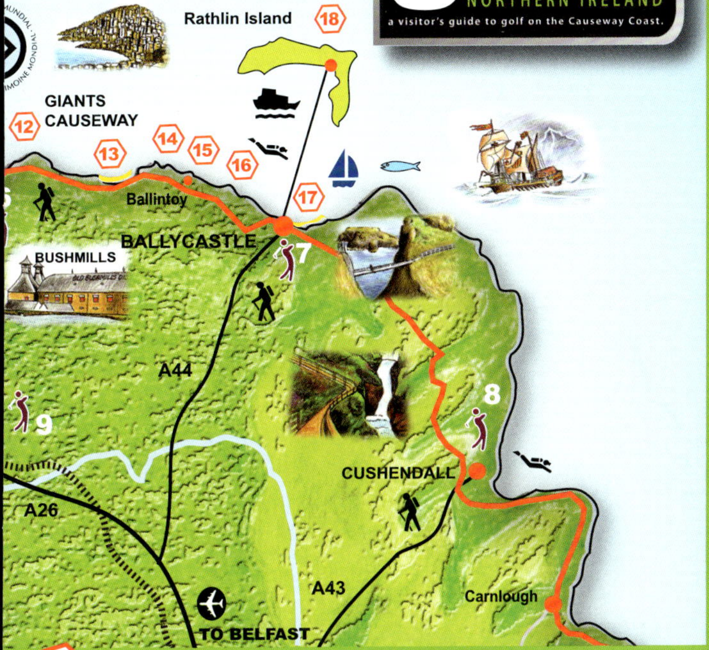

1

Coastal Attractions

1 Magilligan Point, Ferry to Greencastle, Co. Donegal
2 Benone Strand & Benone Golf Course
3 Downhill Strand, Mussenden Temple & Remains
4 Castlerock Golf Club, Castlerock Beach & Trout Fishing
5 Coleraine Historical Town
6 Portstewart Beach, 2 Golf Courses, Cliff Walk, Small Fishing Harbour, Boat Trips & Shore Fishing
7 Ballyreagh 9 Hole Par 3 Golf Course
8 Portrush Peninsula - Ramore Head North, 2 Beaches on East & West sides, Lifeboat Station, North & South Piers, Busy Harbour, Surfing, Diving, Shore & Deep Sea Fishing
9 Dunluce Castle
10 Portballintrae & Bushfoot Golf Club
11 Bushmills, Old Bushmills Distillery
12 Giant's Causeway
13 White Park bay
14 Carrig-A-Rede Rope Bridge
15 Ballintoy & Ballintoy Harbour
16 Dunseverick
17 Ballycastle
18 Rathlin Island

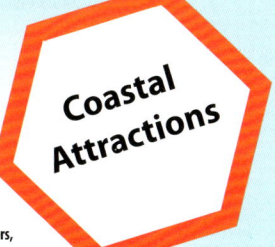

Coastal Attractions

EMERGENCY NUMBERS

Emergency Services
112 or 999 (free)
Non emergency Police number
0845 600 8000 (local rate)
National Health Service - NHS Direct
UK Helpline for Healthcare - 4554
GP Out-Of-Hours -Dalriada Urgent Care
t: (028) 2566 3500

PORTRUSH MAP

Places of interest & useful contact info...

PORTRUSH
Barry's Amusment Park
t: (028) 7082 2340
Beaches - West Strand, East Strand & White Rocks.
Dunlice Castle
t: (028) 2073 1938
North Coast Watersports Centre
t: (028) 7034 4723
Port Path Coastal Walk (Part of the Causeway Coast Way)
Portrush Harbour
t: (028) 7082 2307
Ramore Head Recreation Grounds and Play Park
t: (028) 7082 4441
RNLI Museum and Souvenir Shop
t: (028) 7082 3201
The Arcadia
t: (028) 7082 3924
The Coastal Zone - National Nature Reserve
t: (028) 7082 3600
Royal Portrush Golf Club
t: (028) 7082 2311
Rathmore Golf Club
t: (028)7082 2996

PORTSTEWART
Agherton Old Church
Coleriane Rd, Portstewart.
Portstewart Cliff Path
Part of the Causeway Coast Way
Portstewart Strand
t: (028) 7083 6396
Ringagree Coastal Park
Coastal Walk between Portrush & Portstewart.
Portstewart Harbour
t: (028) 7034 4768
The Cresent Portstewart
t: 078 7988 6005
Portstewart Golf Club
t: 028 7083 2015

COLERAINE
Camus Cross & Bullaun Stone
Curragh Road, Coleraine.
Coleraine Marina
t: (028) 7034 4768
Damhead Minature Railway
t: 077 1402 6864
Mountsandel Fort
t: (028) 2955 6000

Round The Ramparts Heritage Trail
t: (028) 7034 4723
The Phoenix Peace Fountain
Anderson Park, Circular Rd, Coleraine.

CASTLEROCK
Moorbrook Fishery
46 Glebe Road, Castlerock.
t: (028) 7084 9408
Ballyhacket Viewing Point
Ballyhacket Lane, Downhill.
Bishops Gate and Black Glen
Mussenden Road, Downhill.
Castlerock Beach
Sea Rd, Castlerock.
Downhill Demesne & Hezlett House
t: (028) 7084 8728
Downhill Strand
Seacoast Rd, Downhill.
The Giants Sconce
Windyhill Rd, Coleraine.
Castlerock Golf Club
t: 02870 848 314

PORTBALLINTRAE
Portballintrae Harbour
t: (028) 7034 4768

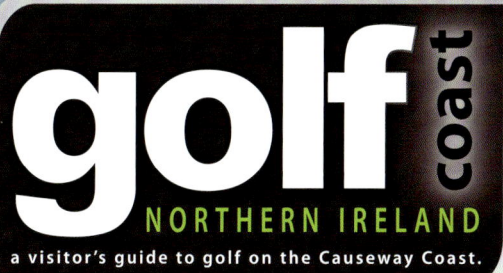

NORTHERN IRELAND

'GOLF CAPITAL OF THE WORLD'

Northern Ireland
Major Home of Golf

'2012-Our time our place', has the Northern Ireland Tourist Board's current advertising campaign theme ever been more appropriate? Tourism and in particular Golf Tourism in Northern Ireland is in the spotlight like never before. So what makes Northern Ireland, a tiny country of not even 1.8m people so important in world golf?

Cast your mind back to 20th June 2010, location: Pebble Beach Golf Links, California and the 110th renewal of the US Open. On the 18th green a Northern Irish Man by the name of Kenny McDowell scuttles across the green to embrace his son Graeme with the words 'You're some kid'. Graeme, of course had just putted out to become the first European to secure victory in a US Open since Tony Jacklin in 1970 and the first Northern Irish man to secure a major since Fred Daly's Open win at Hoylake in 1947.

Fast forward one year later to the 2011 renewal of the same tournament, held at Congressional Country Club, Bethseda, Maryland, when Graeme's close friend and compatriot Rory McIlroy destroys a quality field with a record breaking 16 under par total. Cue back to back victories for Northern Ireland in a tournament that no European had managed to win for forty years! As attention is switched back across the Atlantic to the third Major of the year, the Open Championship, held this year at Royal St Georges in Kent, Northern Ireland's major winners have a new found spring in their step.

This time, for once, the bookies get it wrong, it's not Rory or Graeme who hoists the Claret Jug in the air, but amazingly another Ulster Man, the 2006 European Ryder Cup Hero, Darren Clarke. His five under par total of 275 leaves him three ahead of the tied for second, American duo of Dustin Johnson and Phil Mickelson and makes him the third golfer from Northern Ireland to win a major championship in little over thirteen months. The fact that you have to go back sixty-three years to find the last golfer from here to win one major makes this all the more remarkable.

Northern Ireland, Golf Capital of the world, major home of golf, home of the champions, the superlatives describing these victories are endless, but all very apt. How can a country the size of Northern Ireland produce three major winners in thirteen months? Is it coincidence or is there more to it than that? Well, Darren Clarke has been a stalwart of European golf for years, a veteran of five European Ryder Cup teams and the nemesis of Tiger Woods at the 2000 WGC World Matchplay Championship.

Graeme McDowell has been beating the drum for Northern Ireland on the European and PGA tours since turning pro in 2002, his match winning putt at the 17th green in the 2010 Ryder Cup at Celtic Manor secured yet another remarkable triumph for Europe. And what can we say about Rory McIlroy, 22 years old and already, he's the most talented golfer of his generation. One of the consistently best golfers in the world for the past three seasons, he could go on to dominate the game for years. His victory at the 2012 Honda Classic back in March catapulted him to World Number 1 and reaffirmed Northern Ireland's status as a golfing powerhouse.

So going back to the original question and to quote David Brice of Golf International Inc, why has Northern Ireland been sky-rocketed to golfing glory? As he observes, world class golfers aren't made in heaven, they have to be formed and moulded over time; they need an environment that encourages their basic talent. Brice puts a large slice of this down to the quality of the courses that you'll find here, "Northern Ireland is literally filled with an outstanding collection of top-drawer golf courses, the layouts are simply superb, from some of the best links courses you will ever find, to wonderfully challenging inland layouts that will impress even the most jaded golf traveller".

It's a trait of human nature to take what you have on your doorstep for granted, but David Brice is correct, for the size of our country, the quality of our tracks is pretty awesome. From their amateur days, our golfing heroes grew up playing these wonderful courses, the North of Ireland Amateur championship at Royal Portrush, The Irish Youths at Royal County Down, Clandeboye and Malone and not forgetting over the border, the East of Ireland Championships at Baltray in Co. Louth, the list goes on. Honing their skills around such formidable courses, in perhaps the most testing of conditions is a golfing scholarship in itself, why shouldn't these guys be winning majors?!

If we take our own little corner of Northern Ireland, the Causeway Coast, not many locations can boast such a wonderful array of championship courses within such a small area. From the world renowned links of Royal Portrush, Portstewart and Castlerock to the quaint seaside/parkland hybrid at Ballycastle, not forgetting the inland jewels at Gracehill and Roe Park. The Causeway Coast, a golfing utopia and Northern Ireland's very own Golf Coast!

So, with three major winners in thirteen months, home to the World's Number one golfer, players such as Michael Hoey and Gareth Maybin progressing through the pro ranks and Royal Portrush hosting a major European Tour event for the first time...can things get any better for golf in Northern Ireland?

Arnaldo Morelli

Golf's Holy Grail
Royal Portrush and its links to 'The Open'

The Open Championship 1951

Royal Portrush Golf Club is in the unique position that it remains the only club outside of the United Kingdom mainland that has hosted the Open Championship. 1951 was the year and Max Faulkner's score of 285 (-3) was enough to secure the Claret Jug, surely the most famous and coveted trophy in world golf.

Max Faulkner was a colourful character, born to a club professional in Bexhill-on-Sea, East Sussex; he turned professional after the Second World War and enjoyed several successes throughout Europe. He played in five Ryder Cups, but his career high was winning the Open at Royal Portrush, he described his Open victory as all he had ever wanted.

Faulkner was a fearless competitor who liked to take shots on, this was evident right throughout his victory in '51. One particular shot, at the 16th, during his third round was described by his playing partner, Frank Stranahan as the greatest shot he had ever seen. After hooking his tee shot, his ball ended up a few inches from the out-of-bounds fence. Leading the rest of the field by four strokes, most players would have been sensible and played it safe, chipping it out of danger, laying up and settling for a bogey. Not Max Faulkner. He lashed his 3-wood through the ball and it travelled high over the fence. The gallery watched as it turned right, right again, then bouncing on the fairway it ran on to the green, leaving an easy putt for par. It was typical flamboyance from the English Man.

Max Faulkner made an emotional return to Royal Portrush in 1995, as a spectator, to watch his son-in-law Brian Barnes win the first of his two Senior British Open Championships.

The Early Days

Portrush's links to the oldest and most famous of the four major championships goes back a little further than 1951. The first ever professional competition held in Ireland was played at Royal Portrush back in 1895, the winner was the club's first resident professional, Alex 'Sandy' Herd, the format was match-play and his opponent was a certain Harry Vardon. One year later in 1896, Harry Vardon went on to win the first of his six Open Championships at Muirfield, a record that still stands to this day. Scotsman, Herd was also an Open champion, playing from Huddersfield Golf Club, the club he left Portrush for; he triumphed at Hoylake in 1902.

'image courtesy of Royal Portrush Golf Club'

Did you know? *The Claret Jug has been presented to winners of the Open Championship since 1873.*

Fred Daly
The Father of professional golf on the Causeway Coast

Fast forward to 11th October 1911 and to the birth of Frederick (Fred) Daly. Fred was born and grew up a stone's throw away from the links at Royal Portrush. As a youth he became a much sought after caddy and charged a reputed shilling per round, but he quickly turned his intentions to playing and was often successful in the annual caddie's competition. After serving his apprenticeship under P G 'Stevie' Stevenson at the professional shop in Royal Portrush, his first appointment was resident 'pro' at Mahee Island, on the shores of Strangford Lough.

As a professional, and despite the second world war robbing him of his prime golfing years, he managed to win the Ulster professional championship eight times, the Irish Open once in 1946, he was the first professional Golfer from Ireland to play in the Ryder Cup and then the big one, winning the Open Championship at the Royal Liverpool Golf Club (Hoylake) in 1947. Fred ended up being resident professional at Balmoral, spending the last forty-five years of his life attached to the Belfast club.

After winning the Open, Fred Daly used typical Northern Irish wit in his acceptance speech, as he proclaimed that the Claret Jug would enjoy its first ever visit and a change of air in its new home across the Irish Sea. Fred Daly can be described as the father of professional golf on the Causeway Coast and Ireland; his record of being the only Irish Golfer to win a major championship lasted sixty years and was broken, only by Padraig Harrington's wonderful victory in a play-off against Sergio Garcia at Carnoustie in the 2007 Open.

Daly was a consistent competitor right throughout the late 1940's and early 50's, he played in four Ryder Cups and as well as his success at Hoylake in '47, he finished runner up to Henry Cotton in the 1948 Open, tied second in 1950, fourth in 1951 and third in 1952. Fred Daly's Open winner's gold medal from 1947 takes pride of place in the trophy cabinet at Royal Portrush Golf Club.

***Did you know?** Fred Daly was born and grew up in 76 Causeway Street, Portrush; a few hundred yards from Royal Portrush Golf Club. A blue Ulster History Circle plaque marks the location of the property.*

Fred Daly

'Circa 1950'

Darren Clarke
Open Champion 2011

Darren Clarke was born in Dungannon, County Tyrone, on 14th August 1968, his interest in golf was a natural one; Darren's father Godfrey was head green-keeper at Dungannon Golf Club. He became a junior member of the club and under the tutorage of his father, developed quite a talent for the game. As well as playing on the amateur circuit, winning both the Irish and Spanish Amateur Championships, he also played collegiate golf in the United States for Wake Forest University. Darren joined the professional ranks in 1990 and has been a regular competitor on the European tour since 1991. Darren's affinity with Portrush goes back early in his career. Darren met his first wife Heather in a local nightclub and lived in the town prior to moving to Sunningdale in England. He always retained a property on the North Coast and with his parents moving there too, the Causeway Coast became his adopted Irish home.

Darren's first success on the European Tour came in 1993, with a two stroke victory over Nick Faldo and Vijay Singh, in the Alfred Dunhill Open in Belgium. Since his breakthrough year in '93, he went on to win another twelve tournaments on the European tour. Of his three victories on the PGA tour, his most notable scalp was beating Tiger Woods in the final of the 2000 Andersen Consulting, WGC Match-play Championship. Despite playing in five consecutive Ryder Cups between 1997 and 2006, the 'majors' eluded him. Leading the pack after two rounds in the 1997 Open Championship, a third round score of 71 put him two strokes behind going into the final round, but a final round 65 from American, Justin Leonard, was enough to secure the Claret Jug, leaving Clarke tied for second place.

2011 didn't start too bad for Clarke, the steady form from 2009 and 2010 continued, there were no tournament wins since his KLM Open victory in 2008, but this was about to change. A three stroke win over Chris Wood and David Lynn in Mallorca's Iberdrola Open in May gave Clarke his twenty-first professional tour victory. A nice warm up for the more important tournaments ahead you'd assume, but all didn't go according to plan. In the week before the Open at Royal St Georges, at the Scottish Open, Clarke left Castle Stuart in a fury about how he had putted, in his own words, he wasn't confident that he could birdie anything, unless it was within twelve inches of the hole.

Darren Clarke began the 2011 Open at odds of 150-1, unbeknown to the bookies, on the Tuesday of Open week, Clarke bumped into Bob Rotella, an old friend and golf psychologist, who he had worked with previously and who had worked closely with Padraig Harrington during his own Open victories. Telling him of his woes with the putter, Bob and Darren set to work and going back to basics, quickly developed a rhythm that seemed to work. Prior to each of his four Open Rounds, Darren spent around twenty minutes on the putting green with Bob. Clarke's putting stroke returned with a bang and after two superb opening rounds of 68, he sat tied at the top of the leader board at the half way stage.

A third round 69 eased him ahead, with Dustin Johnston top of the chasing pack, one stroke behind. At the opening hole on Sunday, nerves were eased with a 20-ft putt for par, Clarke doubled his lead at the second, with a birdie and on the third, a Dustin Johnston bogey saw his lead stretch to three, it was a dream start. With an eagle at the par-5 seventh, his fate was sealed, the three shot margin was maintained, Darren Clarke, 140th Open Champion.

Portrush played a big part in Darren's Open victory. Clarke moved back to the North Coast with his two sons, from Sunningdale in 2010, personally, it was a good move. He is now close to his family and Darren has since settled down and got married to former Miss Northern Ireland, Alison Campbell. All those days practicing in the wind and rain at Royal Portrush didn't do his Open chances any harm either, if you can play golf in the wind at Portrush, you can golf play in the wind anywhere. There was quite a party at Royal Portrush when Darren returned from Sandwich with the Claret Jug; sixty four years after the great Fred Daly brought it back from Hoylake. Darren Clarke's Open Winner's Gold Medal now sits next to Fred Daly's, pride of place in the trophy cabinet at Royal Portrush.

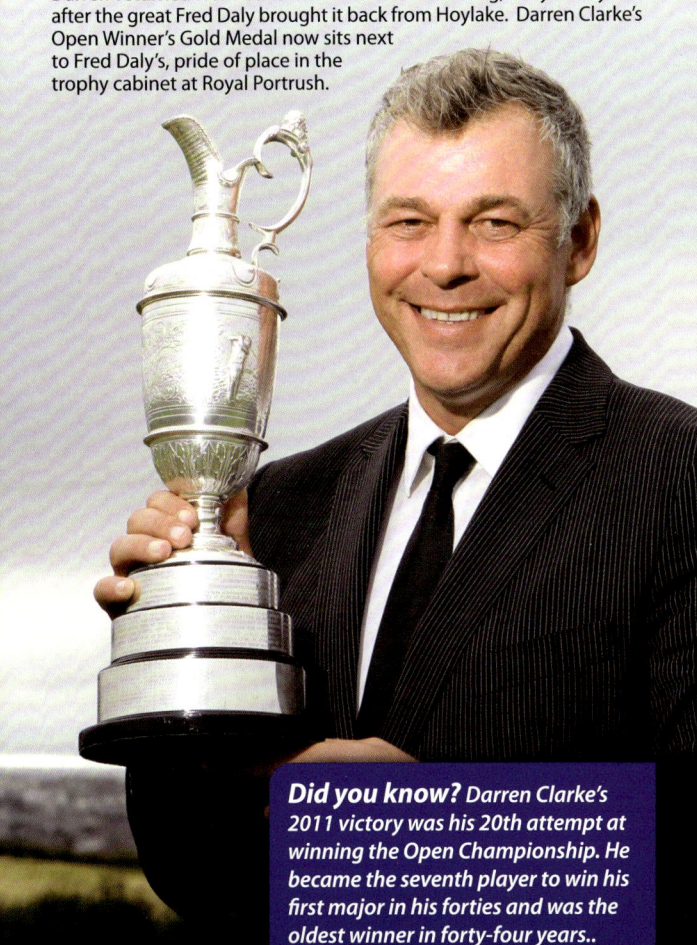

Did you know? *Darren Clarke's 2011 victory was his 20th attempt at winning the Open Championship. He became the seventh player to win his first major in his forties and was the oldest winner in forty-four years..*

The Future

With the story between Royal Portrush and the Open Championship constantly evolving, the question on everyone's lips now, is what lies ahead? For a number of years there have always been mutterings about the Open Championship returning to the Dunluce links one day, but these are usually dismissed as being a pipedream by those in the know. It was said that it was doubtful whether or not the area had the infrastructure to cope with the influx of visitors that an Open attracts. With Northern Ireland's recent successes in the major championships, the issue of the Open returning to Royal Portrush has again been brought to the fore.

Peter Dawson, chief executive of the R & A, organisers of the Open Championship has admitted that with Northern Ireland boasting three recent major winners, it has certainly increased the level of interest in the oldest and most famous 'major' returning to Northern Ireland. After Darren's success in 2011, he pressed Peter Dawson about the possibility of it returning to the North Coast. Clarke has been the perfect ambassador for the Club, describing it as every bit as good as the current Open venues on the R & A's rota. According to former professional and golf course designer, David Jones, it's got nothing to do with the quality of the course, he stresses that it's a well known fact that the Dunluce links is up there with the best courses in the world.

So realistically, what are the chances of the Open returning to the North Coast? St Andrews, Carnoustie and Muirfield are all small seaside locations similar to Portrush, when the Open is played at these locations, spectators stay in hotels as far as Edinburgh and Glasgow. In the 2011 Open, at Royal St Georges, visitors were transported in from all over the south east of England. Northern Ireland is a small country, although there may be a shortage of accommodation in close proximity to Portrush, there is certainly no shortage within a sixty mile radius.

I think the R & A will be watching closely as the European Tour swings into town for the Irish Open in late June and early July. This will be the perfect opportunity to see how Royal Portrush copes with a tournament of this magnitude. With the announcement in February that the course has been chosen by the R & A to host the prestigious British Amateur Championship in 2014, we're all hoping that this just may be a precursor to the return of the Big One.

Arnaldo Morelli

New Kids on the Tee!

Golf Coast Northern Ireland has a chat with one of the stars of the 2011 Great Britain & Ireland Walker Cup team, Paul Cutler.

Profile
Name: Paul Cutler
Age: 23
Home Club: Portstewart Golf Club
Tournament wins/ titles: Ulster boys Championship 2007
East of Ireland Amateur Championship 2009
Nassau Invitational 2009
Lytham Trophy 2010
Irish Close Championship 2011
West of Ireland Amateur Championship 2011
Turned professional: September 2011

Paul was unbeaten throughout the 2011 Walker Cup, winning his two foursomes matches with his compatriot Alan Dunbar. His half against Patrick Cantlay in the final singles match helped GB & Ireland to a 14-12 victory over the USA.

As an amateur, he hit the headlines in the 2011 Irish Open, firing a superb second round 67 to leave him at 6 under, 4 shots behind half way leader Marcel Siem. Paul turned pro in September 2011.

What is the highlight of your career so far?
Playing for Great Britain & Ireland in the successful 2011 Walker Cup team.

What are your golfing goals for the next twelve months?
To earn my right to play on the 2013 European Tour.

What is your favourite course on the Causeway Coast?
Would have to be Royal Portrush, a superb test of links golf.

What is your favourite hole on the Causeway Coast?
The 7th hole at Royal Portrush- it's a very tough hole and requires two great shaped shots to reach the green.

What is the toughest course you've ever played?
Royal Lytham St Annes.

Who is your golfing inspiration/idol?
Tiger Woods

What are your long term golfing ambitions?
To win a Major Championship, I'm not fussy which one.

What one piece of advice would you give a visitor coming to play golf on the Causeway Coast?
Before you play any of the links courses make sure you get plenty of practice in the wind.

Paul Cutler

'Cracking' Northern Ireland

Irish Golf writer Kevin Markham knows the fairways of Ireland like no other, in 2007 he embarked on a journey, in a camper van, that would see him play every 18-hole golf course in Ireland. Here, he reminisces over an eventful round he had on the Causeway Coast.

"What's in it?" I asked, peering at the silver hip flask being offered to me. Tommy had produced it from the depths of his bag on the 12th hole at Castlerock, and after pouring a shot and knocking it back with an exaggerated sigh of contentment, he handed it to me. "Trade secret" he replied with a grin and a raised eyebrow, "but it'll put hairs on your chest."

The sun was out, the sea dazzled in the light and my golfing companions – Tommy, Cedric and Jimmy – had proved entertaining company since they'd invited me to join them on the second hole. Now, Cedric and Jimmy stood with their arms folded watching to see what I'd do. After a pause I reached out and took it. Sure, why wouldn't you! It was one more reason why I was enjoying my Northern Irish adventure, because no matter how you look at it the joy of this island as a golfing destination comes down to three things:

First, the quality of the courses is second to none which is, irrefutably, the key criterion in the destination decision-making process. When you look at the courses dotted along this stretch of northern coastline from Co. Derry to Co. Antrim, it's not hard to see why it is a must-play location.

Second, you've got the weather. True, it's not exactly a key factor when choosing a trip to Ireland, because you could be basking in glorious February sunshine or saving your hotel's water bill by taking soap on to the course for an impromptu August shower. Our weather doesn't have the reliability of Iberia or Turkey, but if you're lucky enough to get a week of perfect sun then you've been blessed, and you can return home with red skin and the knowledge that it's so unexpected there was no suntan lotion in the shops.

And then there's the third reason… a reason that is repeated ad nauseum on advertising campaigns, tourism websites and in guide books… a term so clichéd even the Irish blush with embarrassment. Yes, I'm talking about 'the craic'. We bang on about it so much, tourists expect leprechauns to be directing traffic at motorway junctions, while the girls and boys of Riverdance kick up their heels in every pub in the land to celebrate the rows of Guinness lining the bar.

Here's a little secret… we don't have leprechauns… and there won't be nightly performances of Riverdance, but when you come to Ireland you'll discover that the craic is alive and well… and it's expecting your company in every golf club, restaurant, pub and on every street.

Here's another secret… you don't have to be Irish to enjoy the craic (but it helps!). Simply get into the spirit of things and join in. Whether you're a lone golfer, in a convenient fourball or part of a large group, take a few moments after your round and sit yourself down in the clubhouse bar. Say a few kind words about the course in any direction you choose, and wait for a reply. Someone will surely jump at the opportunity to bend your ear with the club's history, stories of golfing skulduggery or tales that are so tall they are utterly irresistible. You'll learn a lot, laugh a lot and, who knows, you may find yourself whisked off to someone's house for dinner, down to the local bar for some live Irish music, or back on the course for a format you won't understand that involves money you will undoubtedly lose.

The thing is, the craic is about you enjoying yourself, whether you're with your compatriots or having fun with your Irish hosts. It's not a magic formula. It's just the way we embrace life, and the folks of Northern Ireland will do their best to make sure you do the same. Which was why, after being offered the hand of friendship by three Northern Irish golfers I'd never met, it would have been churlish of me to refuse a drink from that silver flask. As the wind snapped around my ankles and chilled my cheeks, I found the deep red liquid seductive and exquisite on the tongue. How did it go down? I can do no more than suggest you take a three iron and hit yourself in the back of the head. It was that good. What's in it? Sorry to say I'm not allowed to tell you, but when you're up this way be sure to ask for some of Bishop Daly's special brew. And believe me, after that you'll discover the craic is truly mighty.

Kevin Markham

You can read about Kevin's Journey around Ireland in *"Hooked, an amateur's guide to the golf courses of Ireland"* published by Collins Press, available from Amazon and all good book shops.

New Kids on the Tee!

Golf Coast Northern Ireland has a chat with 2009 North of Ireland Amateur Champion and recently turned professional Wayne Telford.

Profile
Name: Wayne Telford
Age: 28
Home Club: Rathmore GC Portrush
Tournament wins/ titles: Donaghadee Youths, Aaron Lundy Memorial, North of Ireland Amateur Championship 2009, Arizona Open 2011
Turned professional: January 2012

What is the highlight of your career so far?
That's easy, winning the North of Ireland Championship at Royal Portrush in 2009.

What are your golfing goals for the next twelve months?
I'd like to establish myself on a professional tour and most importantly keep raising my game to new levels.

What is your favourite course on the Causeway Coast?
Royal Portrush, it has 18 fantastic holes that never look the same and it has some of the best scenery in the world.

What is your favourite hole on the Causeway Coast?
The first hole on the strand course at Portstewart, in my view it must have one of the most breath-taking views for an opening hole in world golf and is also a great driving hole for a first tee shot of the day.

What is the toughest course you've ever played?
This would have to be Castlerock GC, a funny choice perhaps, but no matter how well I play there I never go low, I think I need to look at my course management around Castlerock which, by the way is another fantastic course on the Causeway Coast.

Who is your golfing inspiration/idol?
I'm sorry to say it's not Tiger Woods or Rory McIlroy but actually my Dad. In his prime he had a handicap as low as 5, never missed a fairway, was as straight as an arrow and had the temperament of a saint! (laughing)

What are your long term golfing ambitions?
I would like to hold a full European Tour card and to win multiple European Tour events. Also a dream I have always had is to stand on the Swilken Bridge on the 18th at St Andrews with my Dad, something that I hope to fulfill later this year.

What one piece of advice would you give a visitor coming to play golf on the Causeway Coast?
Bring a camera!

Wayne Telford

golf coast
NORTHERN IRELAND
a visitor's guide to golf on the Causeway Coast.

LOCAL HEROES

Looking ahead to the Irish Open, Northern Ireland Golf Reporter Paul Kelly looks at their early season form and profiles three of our home-grown stars.

G-MAC

GOOD old Graeme McDowell, the local boy made good, US Open champion, Ryder Cup hero and part-time match-maker (just ask Darren Clarke). After the highs of 2010 when he won his major at Pebble Beach and claimed the vital point for Europe at Celtic Manor, G-MAC suffered a frustrating 2011.

"I wish you could bottle up the way you feel when golf is easy, because when golf is difficult, it's very difficult," said Graeme on the eve of the Arnold Palmer Invitational at Bay Hill back in March. "I guess I learned a lot of lessons from my 2011 season. I felt like I did a lot of growing up and I went through a process where I acclimatised to being one of the best players in the world, but it was a difficult process to go through".

"I was not focused enough on golf and I was not focused enough on the things that make me tick on a tournament week. I've really got to go out there and kind of nearly not care a little bit. I've got to be well prepared and then prepared to let anything happen that's going to happen. I guess last year my expectations were way too high. I was expecting to go in every week and shoot 66 every day and you just can't do that".

"Your expectation levels crank up and your patience levels crank down, and you have to balance those out. I didn't accept my mistakes last year. I didn't accept hitting bad shots. It's all in the old six inches between the ears. It's a game played in the head for sure."

McDowell went close at Bay Hill, finishing second behind Tiger Woods and then followed that up with a 12th place finish at Augusta. His greatest weapon has always been his mental approach. When he's in the right frame of mind, he's a match for anybody and his Masters performance, when he shot weekend rounds of 71/68 proved just how much his attitude has improved.

"It was a frustrating start to the week, the head was a bit off on Thursday [after an opening round 75] but I realised I had to have an attitude readjustment and I did that," he said.
"I felt a lot more relaxed out there on Friday, Saturday and Sunday and especially on the last two days. I chipped and putted well and gave myself some opportunities".

"I'm very happy with the way I hung in there this weekend. It was another Masters in the books for me and it was fun. These experiences will stand me in good stead going forward. I'd love to pull on a green jacket at some stage in my career and I have to bank experiences and use them going forward. This is only my fifth time at Augusta and your patience levels have to be very high. Mine wasn't on Thursday, but I adjusted quickly and I'll be looking forward to coming back".

Looking forward to a 'wee trip' home in late June...
Imagine teeing off at the 2012 Irish Open, in your home town, on a course that you grew up playing on, around a 9-Iron from where your Uncle first taught you how to swing a club, as a Ryder Cup Star and as the first European to win a US Open for forty-one years.

"Having lived and grown up in Portrush all my life, it's definitely a dream come true to play a tournament of the magnitude of the Irish Open there, I'm going to be very proud to welcome The European Tour to my neck of the woods. The Irish Open has always been one that I've targeted every year. I'd love to win it. I'd love to compete in front of my home fans and pick up the trophy, but to have that at Royal Portrush is extra special for me and there's no doubt it will be highlighted on my schedule. It would definitely be one of the proudest moments of my career. To win the Irish Open at Royal Portrush would be right up there with a Major Championship."

Somebody may be required to pinch Graeme McDowell as he tees up at the first at Royal Portrush on Thursday 28th June 2012, surely this is what dreams are made of? As for winning the tournament, surely it couldn't happen? Or could it?

G-Mac Facts

* *While studying at the University of Alabama at Birmingham, Graeme was ranked Number One Collegiate Golfer in the United States – from 12 starts he won 6 events with a stroke average of 69.6, beating the previous best returned by Luke Donald and Tiger Woods*
* *Won his maiden European Tour title on only his fourth start in the 2002 Scandinavian Masters*
* *Awarded an MBE in the 2011 New Year's Honours List*
* *Also in 2011, Graeme received an honorary doctorate from the University of Ulster*

* *Graeme's recently formed charity; the G-MAC Foundation supports a host of worthy causes including children's medical research in Northern Ireland, Republic of Ireland and the United States*

RORY McILROY

Just how good is Rory McIlroy?

A major winner at 22, ranked world number one at the same age, the lad from Holywood, Co Down has the potential to dominate the game for a decade.

"He is so good for golf. He has so much talent - I have never seen anybody with more talent - and I have played with some great players. It is remarkable," said the legendary South African, Gary Player, in a newspaper interview earlier this year. "Rory is a role model for these times - he is modest and polite. Modern players have to have a sense of responsibility to the game and to the public. And that is what Rory has got. It is going to be so interesting watching him. He is going to be one of those people who stick out."

It is easy to get caught up in the hype that surrounds Rory. He's been a professional golfer for less than five years and is already one of the most marketable names in the game, but he is still finding his feet and learning to make his own decisions. On the course, he remains one of the most exciting players in world golf, but his natural attacking style, so evident in his US Open win, has now been complemented by an improved short game and better course management.

Away from the course, he made significant changes towards the end of 2011 which involved moving to a new management team, Dublin-based Horizon, and committing to the US Tour. Some doubted him, but Rory's form in the early part of the 2012 season has vindicated his decision. A disappointing Masters tournament aside, he has already collected a title, the Honda Classic and contended in many more. His only problem might be keeping a lid on the expectations of fans and 'pundits' who are looking for someone to dominate the game, just as Tiger Woods did for so long.

Thankfully, he remains largely unaffected by the constant attention. He admits that he has had to make some changes to his lifestyle (he can't go out and about as easily as he did in the past), but accepts that as part and parcel of being successful.

"The goals for the season are the same as they have been every year since I turned pro," he said on his return to competitive play this year at the Abu Dhabi HSBC Golf Championship. "I've just tried to improve, just tried to get a little bit better, either at one aspect of the game, or overall, or consistency, or maybe putting in a little bit more work here and there. If I can do that, then hopefully the results will take care of themselves. I'm not really one to set targets, I'd never say I want to win four tournaments this year, or I want to win this, or I want to win that. I'm more focused on the process of trying to become a better player, and if I do that, then obviously that will make it easier to win tournaments."

Will Rory tame the Dunluce Links once again?

Returning home to Northern Ireland to play in a professional tournament with such heritage and expectation as the Irish Open must be an exciting prospect for Rory McIlroy. Revisiting Royal Portrush, the site of that famous course record breaking round of 61, which was achieved during the 2005 North of Ireland Amateur Championships must have the headline writers licking their lips in anticipation.

"For the Irish Open to come to Portrush is a huge thing for any golfer from Northern Ireland. So for myself and the likes of Graeme [McDowell], Darren [Clarke] and Michael Hoey to play the Irish Open in Northern Ireland is a dream come true for us," said Rory. "It's incredible to see the response of the fans so early on, and it just goes to show how popular golf in Northern Ireland has become. I'm expecting huge crowds and a great atmosphere there, and hopefully we can have a memorable week"

"This is going to be one of the biggest events Northern Ireland has ever held, especially as three recent Major Champions will be coming home to play in front of their home fans." Going by advance ticket sales, the Northern Irish public will be out in force in late June and early July to witness the cream of European Golf tackle the famous Dunluce links at Portrush, will it be the young lad from Holywood, County Down who provides the fairytale home win?

Rory Facts
* Youngest ever winner of the West of Ireland Amateur Championship aged just 16
* Recorded a 40-yard drive at age 2 and made his first ace at age 9
* Broke numerous records on his way to winning the US Open in 2011, including the 36-hole tournament scoring record (131), the 54-hole tournament record (199), and the 72-hole scoring record (268)

MICHAEL HOEY

To the uninitiated it may appear that Michael Hoey is something of an 'overnight success'.

In an era of unparalleled glory for Northern Ireland golfers, the 33-year-old claimed three European tour titles inside a 12 month period (May 2011-March 2012).
However, unlike Rory McIlroy, Hoey's rise up the ranks has been littered with false starts and missed opportunities.

Always viewed as a talented player (he won the British Amateur Championship in 2001), Michael struggled to find his feet as a professional golfer. Missed cuts dented his confidence, which in turn raised his anxiety levels. For a long time after turning professional in 2002, it seemed that he might never fulfil his potential.

"The hardest thing when you are not doing well is to see yourself doing well, It's catch-22," said Michael after winning the Trophee Hassan II title in March. "My confidence was knocked a bit trying to find a place on tour. I had periodical highs of winning Challenge Tour events, but I never quite had that consistency."

Michael has four Challenge tour victories to his name, but his breakthrough win came in 2009, when he beat Spain's Gonzalo Fernández-Castaño in a play-off to seal the Estoril Open de Portugal. That victory carried with it a one-year European Tour exemption and freed from worrying about making cuts and earning his place on tour, Hoey has prospered.

In 2010 he failed to win again but he recorded two top tens and made a string of cuts. In 2011 he improved further, winning twice and in the early part of the 2012 season he has already grabbed another tour victory. His form is so good that he is now considered a genuine outsider to book a place on Europe's Ryder Cup team, to defend the trophy in Medinah.

"I was thinking about results too much and constantly thinking about winning. Now I just think about what I need to do on every shot," added Michael. It's no coincidence that Michael's success has coincided with a new period of stability in his life off the course. 'Team Hoey' includes wife Beverley (they married in May 2011), caddy Owen Craig, and Coach Jamie Gough. As a result, he's fit and healthy, more relaxed off the course and looking forward to a summer that includes major appearances (he has automatic entry to the Open Championship) and WGC events.

On the course, he puts his success down to hard work on his short game. "My long game has improved as well, but mainly it's the putting," added Michael. "From a couple of weeks before the Dunhill, I started to putt really well. My stroke has been improving and if you are holing putts it feeds into everything else in your game. I seem to be pretty good when I get into contention. I just need to get there more often. If I do shoot a good score and my name is on the leader board, it actually helps my belief, but I still need to keep working on things."

Looking ahead to the Irish Open at Royal Portrush...

"Killarney last year was an unbelievable atmosphere, with over 80,000 people there and I think there will be crowds like that at Portrush. You can feel the excitement for the event building back home and if we get those kinds of crowds, then it will make the Irish Open feel like a Major. For me, the Irish Open has always been like The Open, and now that it's coming to Portrush, it will be every bit as important as The Open this year. It's an amazing course and with Rory, Graeme, Darren and myself there, it will be a special week for Northern Ireland".

Michael Hoey Facts

* Was a member of the 2001 Walker Cup winning team alongside Graeme McDowell, Luke Donald and Nick Dougherty
* Is a member of Shandon Park golf club (Belfast)
* His victory at Hassan Trophy in Morocco was his third European Tour win in just 25 European Tour events
* He has won over €2 million in European Tour Official Career Earnings
* Has played The Masters as an amateur in 2002 before turning professional (missed cut)

The 'Irish Open'
returns to Northern Ireland's Golf Coast

Irish Golf Correspondent Brian Keogh looks back at the history of the Irish Open and previews the tournament's visit to the Causeway Coast. Northern Ireland has a proud golfing heritage with four major champions - Fred Daly, Graeme McDowell, Rory McIlroy and Darren Clarke – all hailing from the red hand province.

Daly was revered as a golfing god at home for his Open win at Hoylake in 1947 but the current triumvirate are huge international stars, crowd-pullers wherever they go and superb golfing ambassadors for their homeland, and at a time when we take more pride than ever in the prowess of our sporting heroes.
This is a golden age for Irish golf, which looked far afield for its stars for many years before the Daly's, Harry Bradshaw's and Christy O'Connor's of the world blazed an early trail for others to follow.

Ernie Jones, Eddie Polland, David Jones, David Feherty, and Ronan Rafferty would go on to take Northern Irish golf to new heights before McDowell, McIlroy and Clarke followed in Daly's hallowed footsteps with those three major wins in the space of just 13 months. It is a fitting tribute to their achievements that the Irish Open is set to return to the great golfing enclave of Portrush (from June 28 to July 1) this summer, heralding the start of a new era for an event whose history perfectly traces the health of the game on these shores.

Following a successful first staging of the championship at Portmarnock in 1927, there was huge excitement for the 1928 event at Royal County Down where the Open champion Walter Hagen was expected to tee it up. Hagen travelled to Ireland soon after his Open victory to play an exhibition match at Clontarf, promising the Irish Golf Union (as it was known at the time) that he would play in the second Irish Open Championship in Newcastle the following week.

With the exception of Bobby Jones, "The Haig" was probably the world's most famous golfer at the time and his promised participation generated huge interest in the event. However, torrential rain ruined what he had hoped would be a lucrative series of exhibitions at Clontarf and there was consternation when he returned to London and his manager informed the Golfing Union that he would be unable to travel for the Irish Open, citing tiredness as an excuse. The event was still a huge success with Ernest Whitcombe winning by four strokes in sensational weather, earning a cheque for £150 in front of huge crowds. His brother Charles won the title when the Irish Open returned to Northern Ireland in 1930 for its first staging at Royal Portrush.

Ernest would repeat his victory at Royal County Down in 1935, before England's Bert Gadd finished eagle-eagle over the old course lay-out to win at Portrush in 1937. But the event would only be staged a further four times north of the border before it fell into disuse due to financial problems following Scot, Eric Brown's triumph at Belvoir Park in Belfast in 1953. However, the championship was revived by PJ Carroll and Co at Woodbrook in 1975 when Christy O'Connor Jnr heralded the start of a golden era by seeing off the likes of Tom Watson, Jack Newton and Tony Jacklin at the Wicklow venue.

After The Open, it was the second biggest tournament in Europe when it was staged at Portmarnock and Royal Dublin over the next 15 years with major champions such as Ben Crenshaw, Seve Ballesteros, Hubert Green, Bernhard Langer, Ian Woosnam and Jose Maria Olazabal lifting the trophy, before Nick Faldo brought the Carroll's era to an end with the last of three successive triumphs at Mount Juliet in 1993.

Murphy's took over as sponsors from 1994 to 2002 and the event lost some its cachet with just one visit to a links course during that time. Nissan bravely took up the challenge at Portmarnock in 2003, but the changing international scene left the event bereft of big overseas names and following their withdrawal after the 2006 event at Carton House, the event fell into a period of decline.

Played without a title sponsor, Padraig Harrington saved the 2007 edition at Adare Manor with the first victory by an Irish player for 25 years. When the mobile phone company, "3" took over as sponsors at Baltray in 2009, Shane Lowry became the first amateur to take the title. But the communication giants pulled the plug after the 2010 staging in Killarney and while the event struggled on with a decimated prize fund and no sponsor last year, the future looked bleak. However, major wins for McIlroy and Clarke in the US Open and The Open last year, coupled with McDowell's 2010 US Open triumph, accelerated interest in the tournament returning to Northern Ireland for the first time since 1953.

In the aftermath of the celebrations for Clarke's Open win in the summer of 2011, Northern Ireland Tourism Minister Arlene Foster had mooted that negotiations were afoot to bring a major tournament to Portrush in recognition of the trio's exploits, but the belief was that this was to happen in 2013.

Then on 6th January 2012 the official announcement was made by European Tour Chief Executive, George O'Grady, Minister Foster and Open Champion Darren Clarke that Portrush had in fact landed the Irish Open in 2012, a year earlier than everyone had expected.

The excitement shown by the Northern Irish public in the wake of the announcement has led to the European Tour announcing unprecedented interest and a near sell-out in ticket sales at the time of writing. Finally, golf fans in Northern Ireland have a major European tour event to look forward to. Who needs Walter Hagen or even Tiger Woods when you have three major champions in your own backyard?

2011 Irish Open winner, Simon Dyson posing with the Waterford Crystal winner's trophy

Interesting facts:

Tenth Irish Open for Ulster

This year's Irish Open will be the 10th to be held in Ulster and the first since Eric Brown triumphed at Belvoir Park in Belfast in 1953. The event was first held in the north in 1928 when Ernest Whitcombe won the second edition of the championship at Royal County Down, a victory he would repeat at the Newcastle venue in 1935.

Major Pedigree

The Irish Open has a rich history of winners, dating back to 1927. In all, 14 Major Champions have triumphed in the event: George Duncan (1927), Alf Padgham (1932), Reg Whitcombe (1936), Bobby Locke (1938), Fred Daly (1946), Ben Crenshaw (1976), Hubert Green (1977), Seve Ballesteros (1983, 85, 86), Bernhard Langer (1984, 87, 94), Ian Woosnam (1988, 89), José Maria Olazábal (1990), Sir Nick Faldo (1991-93), Michael Campbell (2003) and Padraig Harrington (2007).

Play Offs

Shane Lowry's extra-time victory over Robert Rock in 2009 extended the Irish Open's record for most European Tour play-offs – a total of 11 since the tour's first season in 1972.

Follow Brian Keogh at www.irishgolfdesk.com

The Irish Open takes place at Royal Portrush Golf Club from June 28th–July 1st 2012

Royal Portrush Golf Club, looking forward to welcoming Europe's top golfers at the 2012 Irish Open

artists impression of the buildings at Bushmills Dunes Resort

Bushmills Dunes
An Exciting future addition to Northern Ireland's Golf Coast.

Back in February of this year, Northern Ireland's Environment Minister, Alex Atwood finally granted planning permission for what's surely going to be the most exciting development for golf on the Causeway Coast in well over a Century. The new development, occupying 365 acres of the finest dune-land, close to the Giant's Causeway will include an 18-hole championship golf course, a 120 bedroom resort hotel and spa and 75 golf lodges.

The resort hopes to be operational by 2014. Heading the consortium of US investors who are backing Bushmills Dunes is the New York based Ulster Man, Dr Andrew Hanna, "This is a unique project which will be world class in every aspect. The Dunes are phenomenal. Every Course architect who inspected the landscape has raved about the place. They've said: 'The piece of earth is just made for golf'. It's amazing. There just isn't anywhere else like it in the world"

"With Royal Portrush, Portstewart and Castlerock (golf clubs) in the same area, I want this part of the world to become a golf resort on a par with Pinehurst and Pebble Beach in the USA". Having four world class links courses within half an hour of each other will surely help to establish the Causeway Coast as a golfing destination that would rival anywhere in Europe, if not the world. Dr Hanna adds, that perhaps only St Andrews in Scotland could offer anything like that.

NI Environment minister Alex Atwood inspects the land at Bushmills Dunes

World Class hotel operators, among them, Ritz Carlton and Four Seasons have been approached by the consortium regarding potential involvement in the development, this only goes to strengthen Dr Hanna's plan for Bushmills Dunes to be among the world's top ten golf destinations by 2020. Hanna believes that there is no better time than now to be developing Northern Ireland's golfing profile, "I know this is a difficult time economically, but times will get better. We are not building for today, we are building for tomorrow".

> ***Did you know?*** *Bushmills Dunes course designer, David McLay Kidd is alleged to have told Dr Hanna "If I can't get your course into the world's Top 50 you should shoot me" No pressure there!*

With such a world class, five star resort been developed so close to the Causeway Coast's other golfing gems, this will almost certainly result in Bushmills Dunes being able to attract golfing visitors, who will base themselves in the area for the duration of their vacation rather than them stopping off and playing one or two courses as part of a wider package. It may even be another step towards persuading the Royal & Ancient that the Causeway Coast is ready, once again to host the Open Championship.

Arnaldo Morelli

> ***Did you know?*** *With the resort's close proximity to the UNESCO World Heritage site at the Giant's Causeway, complex designer, Richard Hunter has had to take many environmental issues into consideration. The buildings will be developed along the side of an existing slope and will use local natural stone with grass covered roofing. These features will help the resort's buildings blend in with the local landscape, creating the lowest possible visual impact in such a sensitive area.*

Below: A vista of the land that will occupy the Course at Bushmills Dunes

BUSHTOWN
HOTEL · COLERAINE

Set amidst mature gardens on the outskirts
Of Coleraine, This 3 Star Hotel Offers
38 ensuite bedrooms, Swimming
Pool perfect for Families

'Naturally North Coast' Best Hotel Restaurant
Early Bird Menu, 2 courses for £9.95
'Live Entertainment'
Saturday and Sunday Evenings and Big Band Mondays
15minutes drive to the Beautiful North Coastline & Royal
Portrush Golf Course and 5 minutes away from Coleraine's
Famous Shopping Town

Tel: 028 7035 8367
reception@bushtownhotel.com,
www.bushtownhotel.com

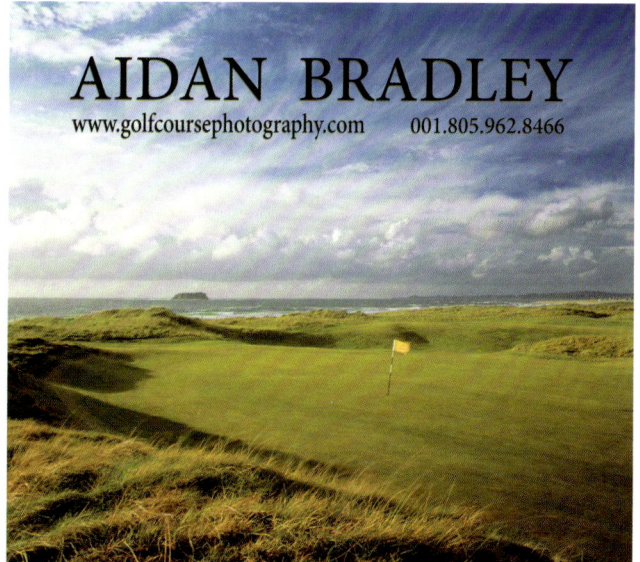

Club Facilities Icon Guide

 Buggies for Hire

 18 Hole Golf Course

 9 Hole Golf Course

 Practice Area

 Trolley Hire

 Motorised Trolley Hire

 Caddies Available

 Driving Range

 Bar & Restaurant

 Mandatory Soft Spikes

 Club Hire

 Pro Shop

 Euros Accepted

 Society Discount

 Dress Code

 Fitness Studio

 Putting Green

 Tuition Available

 Internet Access

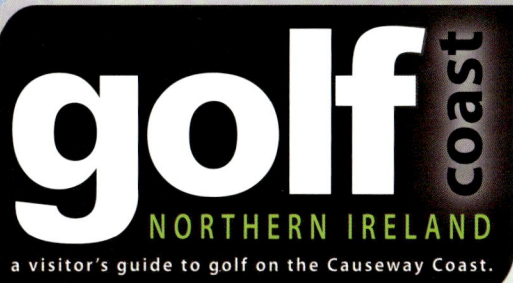

golf
NORTHERN IRELAND
a visitor's guide to golf on the Causeway Coast.

THE COURSES

PROFILES OF EVERY
GOLF COURSE ON THE
CAUSEWAY COAST...

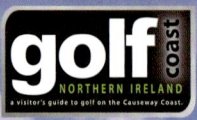

Royal Portrush Golf Club
The jewel in the Causeway Crown

> "It is impossible to overstate the grandeur and the challenge of Royal Portrush. If I had to play only one golf course for the rest of my life, this would be it".
> **John F. Sacks 'Travel & Golf Leisure Magazine'**

6 Dunluce Road
Portrush, Co. Antrim
BT56 8JQ
Tel: +44 (0)28 7082 2311

Web:
www.royalportrushgolfclub.com

Email:
info@royalportrushgolfclub.com

Twitter: @royalportrush

Club Manager/ Secretary:
Wilma Erskine

Club Professional:
Gary McNeill

Course Details

Architect: Harry Colt

Dunluce Links
18 holes Par 72 7143 yards
(Handicap certificate required)

Course Record:
Rory McIlroy 61

Valley LInks
18 holes Par 70 6304 yards

Course Facilities:

Club History

On the 21st of April 1888, around thirty men met in the Northern Counties Hotel, Portrush, their intention was to secure some land, with the hope of developing the game of golf in the resort. A committee was formed and a Mr John Staples Alexander from Portglenone was elected the first Captain of the County Club, as it was first known.

Honorary Secretary (pro temp) was a Mr George L Baillie, an English teacher, based at Belfast Royal Academy, who hailed from Musselburgh near Edinburgh. He is largely credited with introducing the game of golf to Ireland and was one of the founders of the Royal Belfast Club. They quickly secured a parcel of land close to the railway station on a long lease; it was known locally as the large triangle and was owned by the Earl of Antrim. The course was to have 9 holes, but no club house. The course was formally opened on Saturday 12th May 1888 and the occasion was marked by forty players competing for one scratch prize and four handicap prizes; the silver cup that they competed for was won by George Baillie. By September 1888, the membership of the club numbered seventy and had an annual subscription of one guinea. As early as New Year's Day 1889, it was reported that a new nine holes had been constructed close to the original nine.

Did you know? *Only for a late amendment to a motion put forward at a special general meeting in 1895, Royal Portrush Golf Club was set to be known as the Royal St Patrick's Golf Club.*

'photo courtesy of Royal Portrush Golf Club'

In May 1889, new plans for a further 18 holes located to the east of the resort had been made. It was reported in the Belfast News Letter that "Old Tom" Morris was to be involved in the design of the new layout. After visiting the course to play a match, he made some suggestions and was set to return later in the year, but it never materialised. After securing the extra land to the east, from the Earl of Antrim, the development of a further 18 holes went ahead and by October 1890, the club had two 18-hole courses.

By 1891, it was agreed that when membership reached 300, the entrance fee would be raised from one guinea to three, this was to help secure another tract of land to the East and also to cover the construction costs of a brand new clubhouse. By the end of 1892 the club had grown significantly, with membership now numbering 370. With the help of the club's second captain, Captain James Martin McCalmont, M.P. for East Antrim, the County Club became known as the Royal County Club, when Prince George, the Duke of York agreed to become its patron. The reputation of the club grew further and in 1895, it changed its name to Royal Portrush Golf Club, The Prince of Wales, later to become King Edward VII became its new Patron.

In 1896 the club started to develop the lands that they acquired on the eastern side of the resort, the dune land started at the bottom of the Bushmills Road and ran all the way to the White Rocks, with further additions made in 1909, this became known as the 'long course'. This course proved to be the most popular with visiting golfers and it quickly became known as the championship course. Large parts of the long course were controlled by the Railway Company, who leased the land from Lord Antrim and in effect sub-let it to the club. The lands were often in dispute and it wasn't until 1928, that the new Earl of Antrim granted a 99-year lease for all Lord Antrim's lands to the Club.

Club History (cont)

This was quite a coup for Royal Portrush; negotiations were conducted on behalf of the club by Sir Anthony Babington and the then captain, Daniel McLaughlin, a solicitor from Coleraine. Sir Anthony was a prominent lawyer, who practiced at the bar, first in Dublin, then later in Belfast. He was born in Londonderry and was a member of the North West Club at Lisfannon, in his university days he'd often come along to play the links at Royal Portrush. In 1923 Sir Anthony became involved in the council of the club, Daniel McLaughlin, Sir Anthony and a handful of others were seen as the go-ahead members of the council.

By securing further 99-year leases from two prominent local land owners in 1931, the club now had control of approximately 80 acres of pure, undulating, links land, just waiting to be developed. It was as early as 1923, when Sir Anthony Babington first brought over to Portrush, Mr Harry S Colt, the prominent golf course architect and designer, to lay out plans for two 18-hole courses, both set close in to the sand hills. Remarkably, it wasn't until June 1932, nine years after his original visit, that the tenure of the land had been secured and the council of the club were in a position to approve Mr Colt's plans. Colt's final lay out for the Dunluce Links was said to be completed and presented to the club in 1929.

Work commenced immediately and was completed swiftly enough for the course to be played on the following Easter, the official opening was carried out a little time later, in July of 1933, by the Lord Mayor of London, Sir Percy Greenaway. The final hole of the Dunluce links is named in his honour.

Did you know?

In the 1919 Irish Amateur Open at Royal Portrush (the first held after the Great War), a Mr T.D Armour from Lothian Burn was defeated in the final.

Shortly afterwards Tommy Armour turned professional and emigrated to the USA, becoming a household name by winning the US Open in 1927 and the British Open in 1931.

Rathmore Golf Club History

Rathmore Golf Club probably existed before this date, but the first mention of the club comes from the minutes of a meeting held at Royal Portrush in 1947, at this meeting, permission was granted for Rathmore to apply for membership to the Golfing Union of Ireland and therefore, become a recognised club in its own right.

The town or 'privileged' players as they were known were mostly non-professionals, who hailed from the harbour end of Portrush, this area is known as Ramore, hence the origins of the club's name. Although membership was open to all residents of the town, the reason they were 'privileged' was because approval was needed from the Royal Portrush Club, before their membership was granted.

Although the Valley links is looked after by Royal Portrush Golf Club, the Rathmore club act as its custodians. The Club is credited with producing some of the finest golfing talent in the Causeway Coast area, including 1947 Open Champion, Fred Daly; U.S Open Winner, Graeme McDowell; recently turned professional, Wayne Telford and 2010 Irish Open, Amateur champion and 2011 Walker cup star, Alan Dunbar.

Harry Colt

"Mr H.S. Colt... has thereby built himself a monument more enduring than brass"

Writer, Bernard Darwin, commenting in the Times, prior to covering the 1951 Open at Royal Portrush.

Henry Shapland "Harry" Colt is probably the finest golf course architect that ever lived; he was born in Highgate, England in 1869. He completed a law degree at Cambridge University and captained the University Golf Club in 1889. Despite being a practicing lawyer, the draw of golf got the better of him. He was a founding member of Rye Golf Club in East Sussex, helping to lay out the course and then becoming honorary secretary for a few years. At the turn of the century, he moved on to a brand new club, Sunningdale, in a management capacity, but his real love was course architecture.

After several more management positions, he decided, just prior to the Second World War, to go into golf course design in a full time capacity. Working with partners, Charles Alison and John Morrison, they were responsible for the construction, design and re-modelling of over three hundred courses. These include Muirfield, Hoylake (Royal Liverpool) and Sunningdale in the U.K. and Pine Valley, Cypress Point and Augusta (with Bobby Jones) in the USA. Harry Colt, himself, was responsible for one hundred and fifteen of these. In 1928 they formed the company, Colt, Alison and Morrison Ltd; Harry Colt remained managing director until his retirement in 1945.

Despite Muirfield being one of his earlier projects, Harry Colt felt that Royal Portrush was his greatest ever achievement. It is a testament to the man that since 1910, the Open Championship has been played on a Colt designed course, no less than forty-seven times.

'all images courtesy of Royal Portrush Golf Club'

Intro

The seaside town of Portrush occupies a peninsula on one of the most northerly points of the Antrim Coast. Flanked by two superb sandy beaches, one to the west (West Bay) and the Curran strand, that leads to the White Rocks on the East. The resort gained popularity as a holiday destination in Victorian times and can trace its golfing heritage back to the late 1800's.

Royal Portrush Golf Club takes up a position to the east of the resort and is spread out over a large triangle of sand dunes, there are two 18-hole courses, the championship; Dunluce links, taking its name from the 13th century castle ruins, that overlook the course (the only course in Ireland to host the British Open) and the Valley links, as its name suggests, set in a valley just below the championship course. Legendary architect, Harry Colt is responsible for the layout of both courses.

It would be difficult to find a grander entrance to any golf property than that of Royal Portrush. Driving from the south, either on the B62 or the stunning A2 coastal route, turning the bend into Portrush, the two links courses unravel before your eyes, a green, lunar-like landscape set amongst the dunes, a golfing utopia with the north Atlantic breakers crashing on the beach below. The scenery here is simply stunning and offers some of the most awe-inspiring and spectacular views on the island.

What they say! *"I would love to see a British Open round here one day. Royal Portrush's Dunluce links is a far better course than Troon. This is one of the real great Open courses".*
Golfing legend and 10 times Major winner, Gary Player.

intro cont

The Dunluce course, host to the 2012 Irish Open, is renowned as being one of the world's finest links courses, regularly making the top twenty in the world's top 100 course lists, as Golf World describes it, "Royal Portrush is a must-play stopover for golfers eager to experience one of the toughest golf challenges there is". The Valley links is shorter, but still provides visitors with a supreme round of true links golf.

The undulating greens, mounded fairways and un-forgiving rough, coupled with high winds, that can change direction, almost by the minute, make these links courses formidable tests, even for the low handicap golfer. Accurate driving between the narrow fairways is a must here, there are very few bunkers at Royal Portrush, but don't let that lull you into a false sense of security, it doesn't need them. There are enough natural hillocks and mounds among the dunes to ensure, that with one awkward bounce, it will send a wayward tee shot into lots of places that you'd prefer not to be.

The Courses
The Championship Dunluce Course

It's a well stated fact, that when the British Open was held here in 1951, only two players managed to break 70. Royal Portrush's Dunluce course is one of the toughest links courses on the planet, eighteen glorious holes that undulate and weave their way through some of the finest, natural, dune-land that exists anywhere.

The setting is magnificent, the view from the elevated tee at the 5th, followed by the walk down to the green towards the ocean offers some of the most spectacular scenery that you're ever likely to encounter on a golf course, directly below is White Rocks Beach, look to the right and perched high on a cliff, you'll see the rugged ruin of Dunluce Castle, to which the course takes its name. With the Donegal headlands to the west and the Scottish Isles visible to the north east, at times it can be difficult to concentrate on the golf, but concentrate you must.

Hole number & name	Championship yardage	Par	Stroke Index
1 Hughies	416	4	7
2 Giant's Grave	528	5	11
3 Islay	174	3	17
4 Fred Daly's	479	4	3
5 White Rocks	411	4	9
6 Harry Colt's	189	3	15
7 P.G Stevenson's	431	4	1
8 Himalayas	433	4	13
9 Tavern	475	5	5
Out	3536		
10 Dhu Varren	478	5	10
11 Feather Bed	191	3	18
12 Causeway	412	4	2
13 Skerries	418	4	6
14 Calamity Corner	210	3	16
15 Purgatory	391	4	12
16 Babington's	442	4	4
17 Glenarm	581	5	14
18 Greenaway	484	4	8
In	3607		
Out	3536		
Total	7143		

The Dunluce course begins with a short, uphill, Par-4 with out-of-bounds on either side, the Par-5 2nd offers the first fairway with a slight bend, in fact seven holes on the Dunluce links are dog-legs, with fairways that all take a marked change of direction, a somewhat unique feature for a links course. The first feature hole of the front nine is the Par-4 4th, according to 'Golf Club Atlas' this is one of the best 'un-known' holes in the world, out of bounds to the right with deep bunkers in the centre of the fairway; the green is tucked neatly into the dunes.

The par-4 5th (White Rocks), isn't just renowned for its inspiring views, this is one tough hole, short in distance at 411yards; it takes a dog leg right, around 220yards. An aggressive drive, shortening the dog leg, if accurate, will be rewarded by a much shorter, but by no means easier, approach. The green is in a precarious position, right on the cliff edge, to the right, there is a large hollow and to the left, a deep bunker. The par-3 6th presents a difficult shot to get the ball to the back of the two-tiered green and is followed by what is rated the toughest hole on the course, the par 4 7th.

> ***Did you know!*** *Royal Portrush's Dunluce links is treble 'major' winner, Padraig Harrington's favourite golf course.*

The back nine begins with the longish, par-5 10th, a tough hole, especially when the wind blows. The hardest rated hole on the homeward stretch is the par-4 12th (Causeway). Straightforward in appearance, the green slopes down on all sides and is protected by a hidden 12-foot bunker along the left, avoid this at all costs. Prior to the signature 14th, the par-4 13th, requires a blind tee shot towards the crest of the dune, a downhill approach to the green offers a superb view of the Skerries, a small group of rocky Isles, just off the shore.

After negotiating the chasm at Calamity Corner (14th), you are presented with another dramatic hole, the par-4 15th, aptly named 'purgatory'. This requires a straight drive down the narrow fairway, the green undulates in many directions and is surrounded by bunkers; accuracy is the key here. The par-4 16th is another dog-leg, left to right and this is followed by the longest hole on the course, the par-5 17th. 18 is a fine closing hole that contains no less than eleven bunkers (20% of the bunkers on the entire course). It was made famous in 1997, when Gary Player struck a fine 3-wood, setting up a birdie to help him win the Senior British Open Championship.

Did you know?
Max Faulkner tempted fate and signed autographs, as 'Open Champion 1951' prior to the final round being played, at that stage he was six shots ahead and ended up labouring to a two shot victory over runner up, the Argentinian, Antonio Cerda.

Course Map

Dunluce Links

Valley Links

Featured Hole:
14th Hole "Calamity Corner" (Dunluce Course)

This 210 yard, par-3 is one of the most famous holes in golf, between the tee and the green there is a large ravine that must be cleared to have any chance of securing your 3. Standing on the tee, looking at the small target on the cliff ahead, there is no mistaking, that a brilliant shot is required to ensure a successful conclusion to this hole. Your shot will require a long carry, go right and you'll watch your ball roll and bounce down the steep chasm towards the valley links below, therefore succumbing to a double bogey at best. Good luck.

What they say? *"Calamity Corner is the hardest par 3 I've ever seen, it plays 210 yards, uphill and into the wind to a green on the side of a cliff. I retired to the upstairs bar…and began the slow process of returning to our accustomed selves – the ones who play the ordinary, earthbound kind of golf."*
Charles McGrath, New York Times

Famous Visitors:
Golfing legends; Gary Player, Arnold Palmer, Tom Watson, and Jack Nicklaus.
Major winners; Ernie Els, Larry Mize, Phil Mickelson, Jim Furyk, Mark Calcavecchia, Davis Love lll, Steve Jones, Tom Kite and Ben Crenshaw

Famous Members:
Graeme McDowell
Darren Clarke
Padraig Harrington

Did you know? The present Royal Portrush club house was completed in 1999 at a cost of £1.5m and was officially opened by HRH The Duke of York, Prince Andrew.

Did you know? Royal Portrush led the way for ladies golf in Ireland. In the late 1800's and early 1900's two lady members, May Hezlet and Rhona Adair won 5 British Ladies Open Amateur championships between them.

The Valley Links

Living in the shadow of its illustrious neighbour and big brother, the Valley course is mistakenly, often overlooked by visiting golfers. Slightly shorter than the Dunluce Course, this makes the Valley a little less demanding, but it's by no means any less of a challenge. The Valley shares the familiar traits of the Dunluce Course; tight narrow fairways, a fair share of bumps, hollows and undulations, stunning links greens and a need for total accuracy off the tee.

The Valley links is laid out between the towering dunes that flank the East Strand beach and the raised land to which the Dunluce Course occupies. Historically known as the 'War Hollow', the large dunes enclose the course, blocking out the extreme elements to a degree, intriguingly, some of the holes are actually below sea level. Many of the greens are small and are tucked neatly into the dunes. The relatively small number of bunkers is again, a testament to the quality of the natural links land that the course is set out on.

The two stand-out holes on the Valley course are back-to-back in the front 9. The short par-4 5th (Desert) is set in its own natural valley and is played from an elevated tee set in the sand hills to a green surrounded by towering dunes and flanked on three sides with deep, menacing bunkers. The longish, par-3 6th is played slightly uphill, to a green with its right hand edge obscured by a section of dune. A bunker, short and left of the green and a steep drop off the apron, provide potential hazards.

What they say? *"A sheltered quality, an attractive snugness, if you will, characterises the course. The Valley Course is full of very good golf holes. Even accomplished players are challenged and all of us are charmed"*
James W Finegan, Where golf is great – The finest courses of Scotland and Ireland.

Advice from the Pro!

Golf Coast Northern Ireland has a chat with Royal Portrush Golf Club Assistant Professional, Michael McCrudden

Name: Michael McCrudden

Occupation/ Position: PGA Assistant Professional, Royal Portrush Golf Club

Course Summary: The Dunluce Links is a challenging but fair Championship course. Set amongst towering sand dunes and the breathtaking scenery of the North Coast, it is a must play course for any golfer. Every hole has a unique feel and the course places an emphasis on careful shot selection and straight driving.

My 3 tips for a visitor playing Royal Portrush Dunluce Course for the first time:

1) Practice some links style shots before you play. The 'bump and run' is a necessity around the links and you will need this shot if you are looking to tidy up around the greens. If the wind is blowing, go to our range before your round and work on the low shot, this can be an invaluable shot to use once you are out on the course. Remember, the harder you swing it, the more the ball will spin and the higher it will go, so swing easy!

2) Bring the right kit. With the ever changing weather it is important to be prepared for all seasons. Check the forecast before you come to play and if it's going to be cold, layer up. A base layer, shirt, and jacket are much easier to play in than a bulky top. If it's going to be warm, bring sun cream and use water to stay hydrated, this will keep you going right to the eighteenth hole.

3) Get some local advice. Speak to the Professional staff about how the course is going to play on the day, as they will be able to tell you which holes to go for, or where you should lay up. A caddy or a course guide will also give you some ideas on what to expect on each hole as you play. The best advice for Dunluce is once in trouble, make sure and get out of it!

Michael McCrudden

DUNLUCE GOLF SHOP
All your golfing needs at internet prices!

Dunluce Golf Shop
Unit 25, causeway Enterprise Agency,
Loughanhill Industrial Estate, Coleraine, BT52 2NR
Tel: +44 (0)28 70 55 8382 or 084 4847 9808
email: enquiries@dunlucegolf.com
www.dunlucegolf.com

www.dunlucegolf.com
Golf

ARMSTRONG GORDON
THE PROFESSIONAL PROPERTY AGENT [Est. 1947]

Own **your** piece of Northern Ireland's Golf Coast!

The market is moving... **Are you?**

64 The Promenade, Portstewart, BT55 7AF.
(028) 7083 2000   www.armstronggordon.com

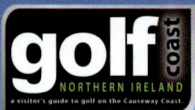

Portstewart Golf Club
'The Causeway Coast's second in command'

"The whole front nine at Portstewart, ambling its way between the dunes and then out along the river, is an unfurling scroll of one outstanding hole after another".
Charles McGrath 'New York Times'

117 Strand Road
Portstewart
Co. Londonderry
BT55 7PG
Tel: +44 (0) 28 70 832015

Web:
www.portstewartgc.co.uk

Email:
bill@portstewartgc.co.uk

Club Manager/Secretary:
Michael Moss

Club Professional:
Alan Hunter

Course Details

Architect:
A G Gow & Des Giffin

Strand Course
18 holes Par 72 6912 yards

Course Record:
66 Adam Brown

Riverside Course
18 holes Par 68 5725 yards

Old Course
18 holes Par 64 4822 yards

Course Type:
Links

Club History

Although the club was officially formed a few years later, Portstewart can trace its golfing heritage back to 1889. It was Boxing Day and a group of locals led by Coleraine solicitor, Dave McLaughlin organised a tournament, hoping to attract visitors who were attending the Christmas meeting at the neighbouring County club at Portrush. The competition was a fantastic success and showed competitors that the golfing ground at Portstewart was as good as what was being used by the club further along the Coast at Portrush.

The land being used followed the shoreline just outside Portstewart and flanked the County Road that connected the resort with Portrush; these lands were owned by the Cromore Estate. Mr R.A.C Montagu whose family controlled the estate was a founding member of the club and was elected the first captain in 1894, he later became the first ever club president. Like many others, the course was originally 9 holes and was spread over 26 acres, the official yardage according to the Irish golfer's Annual of 1897 was listed as 1495 yards.

Despite the original course been extended first in 1904 and later in 1918 and 1934, membership was growing and the present facilities were deemed not to be sufficient. At a special meeting in 1907, after having secured land at the opposite end of the town close to the Strand, members approved the building of a new 18-hole course. The design and layout was trusted to a Mr A.G Gow of Portrush and the first tournament was held in July 1908. A cottage, close to the road was converted for use as a clubhouse and the club transferred all its activities to this new site.

The famous Scottish course architect, Willie Park Jnr completed a makeover in the 1920's and excluding some alterations in the 1960's, the course remained largely unchanged, until Des Giffin's modern day re-design extended the course into the 'Thistly Hollow' in the 1990's.

Portstewart's Strand Course is a championship course in every sense of the word. It has played host to many important tournaments over the years. The first tournament of note was the Irish Native professional golf championship in 1931; this returned under the auspices of the IPGA Championships in 1974 and was won by Eddie Polland, who set a course record of 66 around the old strand course.

> *Did you know?* ? *One of the finest golfers that Portstewart ever produced was BBC Golf commentator Maureen Madill. Winner of the British ladies Amateur Golf Tournament in 1979 and the British Ladies Amateur Stroke play tournament in 1980 she went onto represent GB and Ireland in the 1980 Curtis Cup.*

The prestigious Irish Amateur Close Championship has been held twice in 1960 and 1992. Ladies golf championships also figure strongly with the British Ladies seniors taking place in 2004 and the British Girls Championship in 2006. Perhaps most famously, Portstewart's Strand course hosted the qualifying rounds for the 1951 Open that was held at Royal Portrush.

Club Intro

Portstewart is located along the coast, approximately three miles to the west of Portrush. Whilst Portrush has all the hussle and bussle, Portstewart can be described as having a more tranquil and sedate vibe. The focal point of the town is the Promenade, with its gift shops, cafes and ice cream parlours, this leads to a two mile stretch of golden sands, known as Portstewart Strand. Towering sand dunes overlook the Strand and behind these, are two of the three 18-hole courses that make up Portstewart Golf Club. The club, one of the few 54-hole complexes in Europe was founded in 1894.

The three courses are known as the Strand Course, taking its name from that stretch of beach that lies beyond the dunes next to the course, the Riverside Course, part of which meanders along the River Bann, as it makes its way out into the Atlantic Ocean and the old Course, that sits at the opposite end of the town in an area known as Portmore and so named, because it was the original location for Golf in the resort, locals call this the 'Town Course'.

Part of the land that makes up the current Strand and Riverside Courses was originally an 18-hole course that provided a dual golfing experience, with the opening nine holes set into the dunes and providing a classic links experience, and the closing nine, more of an inland nature. Expansion was carried out in the 1960's and again in 1992, when a further area of dunes

"How good is the strand course at Portstewart? For my money, just one rung below County Down and Portrush and under no circumstances to be missed".
James W Finegan
'Where golf is great-the finest courses of Scotland and Ireland'

known as the 'thistly hollow' was purchased. This extension to the Strand Course was designed by Portstewart member and local school teacher, Des Giffin and resulted in the creation of one of Ireland's finest links courses.

The Strand course has all the traits of a true Irish links, mounded fairways set tight into the dunes, lightening fast greens (all year round) and stunning natural scenery. Portstewart is a membership based club that offers a warm welcome to visitors. The newly built (2009) clubhouse is an imposing building with fantastic views over the course and offers superb bar and restaurant facilities.

The 18-hole Riverside Course is made up of the old back nine of the Strand Course prior to the changes in 1992, so it has more of an inland, leisurely feel; the holes along the banks of the River Bann are particularly scenic. The Old Course at Portmore hugs the rocky shoreline and offers visitors an old fashioned seaside golf experience, a gentle introduction perhaps, compared to the tougher challenges that lie ahead.

What they say! ? *"The designer has created a number of incredible holes, and deserves credit for ensuring that the new holes assimilate subtly and smoothly with the originals, Portstewart is at the heart of a magnificent Northern Irish Golf Tour"*
www.yourgolftravel.com

The Courses
The Strand Course

Des Giffin's extension into the Dunes at Portstewart has created one of the finest links courses, not just on the Causeway Coast, but in the whole of Ireland. Top100golfcourses.com describes the Strand Course as exhilarating, incredibly challenging and thoroughly enjoyable, with one of the best opening nine holes in golf.

Standing on the Signature, first tee at the Strand Course, it would be impossible not to be inspired. It's widely acknowledged that the 1st at Portstewart is the finest opening hole in Irish Golf, some would say Europe. Resident professional, Alan Hunter sums it up pretty well in the course planner, his advice – don't look up until you've hit your first shot.

Hole number & name	Championship yardage	Par	Stroke Index
1 Tubber Patrick	427	4	11
2 Devil's Hill	366	4	7
3 The Settlement	218	3	13
4 Thistly Hollow	538	5	5
5 Rifle Range	461	4	1
6 Five Penny piece	143	3	15
7 Strawberry Hill	516	5	17
8 Portnahapple	427	4	3
9 Larkhill	361	4	9
Out	**3457**		
10 Fisherman's Walk	407	4	10
11 Fernside	407	4	4
12 Barmouth	167	3	18
13 Cashlandoo	498	5	16
14 The Hill	493	5	12
15 Articlave	168	3	14
16 The Plateau	418	4	6
17 Agherton	436	4	2
18 Strand Head	461	4	8
In	**3455**		
Out	**3457**		
Total	**6912**		

Hole 2 – Devil's Hill, is just as dramatic, snaking its way through the giant dunes that run the whole length of the narrow fairway. A little respite is offered at the 3rd, the first par-3, a challenging 218 yard, single shotter. The par-5 4th brings you into the heart of the 'thistly hollow', a slight dogleg right with a fairway full of bumps and undulations. Hole 5, the aptly named rifle range, with its narrow fairway is ranked as the hardest hole on the course, the green is protected by the narrowest of entrances, legendary course designer; Robert Trent Jones described it as "easy bogey, tough par".

The par-3 6th, Five Penny Piece (taking its name from the plateau green that slopes down on all sides) will last long in the memory, it requires supreme accuracy and offers dire consequences if this isn't achieved. Two severe dog legs at holes 7 and 8 (with 8 being a blind tee shot) lead you to the 9th-Larkhill, described by resident pro, Alan Hunter as the best 350yd par-4 in the country.

> **Did you know?** *Whilst many clubs spend millions on extensions and re-designs, the most recent work at Portstewart was all undertaken internally, the new holes were designed by member Des Giffin and the work was undertaken under the watchful eye of course manager, Bernard Findlay.*

The back nine begins with the 407 yard par-4 10th and guides you inland towards the upper banks of the River Bann, the ground here is a little flatter, but is still pure links and retains all the bumps and hollows of the front nine. The elevated tee of the 11th offers superb views of the river twisting its way out towards the Atlantic Ocean.

Hole-14 (par-5) with its narrow entrance to the green and unforgiving rough can punish the big hitters, maybe best to play it safe and accept your par here. Five bunkers protect the green at the par-3 15th, to avoid a bogey, ensure that you steer clear of these.

Holes 16-18 are the most exposed on the course, but are all excellent (and extremely tough) par-4's, the view down to the strand is uninterrupted, so when the wind is blowing, these holes in particular can play a lot longer and harder, with these elements coming into play, choose your club carefully.

Portstewart's Strand Course will surprise many visitors to the Causeway Coast, it doesn't boast the reputation of its 'Royal neighbour' and this, perhaps plays to its strengths, this is one seriously good links course, with what many regard as having some of the finest opening holes in world golf. The greens are quick all year round, the terrain is as tough as it comes, be prepared to play links golf in one of its purest forms. .

Course Map

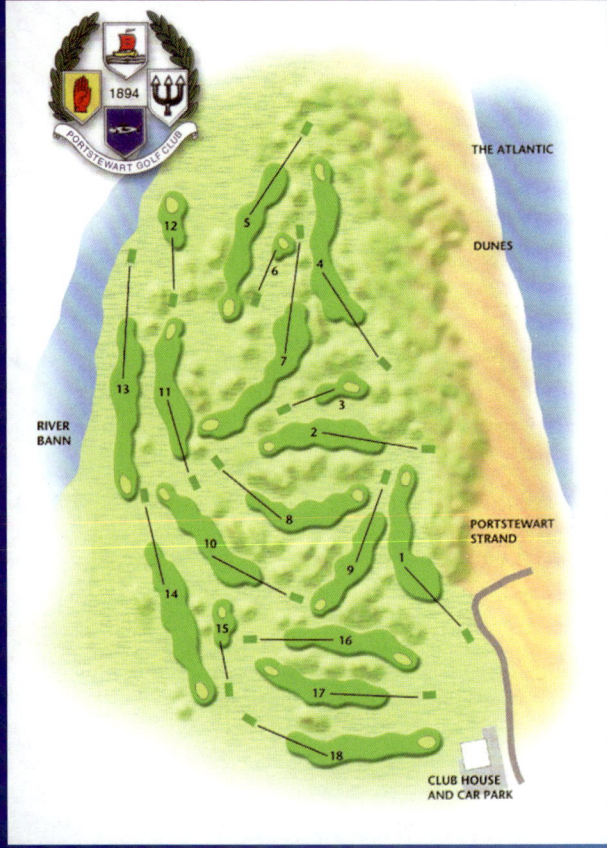

Featured Hole:
1st Hole "Tubber Patrick" *(Strand Course)*

The views from the opening hole of the stand course are a sight to behold. The dunes rolling down onto the beach below, surfers riding the white tops as they break close to the shore, the Barmouth; where the River Bann enters the Atlantic Ocean, the Mussenden Temple on the cliff top at Downhill and beyond this, the gaping entrance to Lough Foyle, with the headlands of Donegal's Inishowen peninsula casting a shadow, in the distance.

This hole isn't all about the scenery, the tee occupies an elevated platform and you're hitting downhill into the towering dunes below. The hole is 427 yards from the blue championship tee with a dog leg right to the green, a stunning opening hole that sets the scene for what lies ahead.

> ***What they say?*** *"The first hole of the Strand Course is an absolute stunner, one of golf's most intimidating, a downhill 425 yard par-4."*
> **Top 100 Golf Courses-Course Review.**

Famous Visitors:

Legendary Miami Dolphins quarterback Dan Marino
Davis Love III

The Riverside Course

Compared to the Strand Course, the Riverside course offers a less challenging, more tranquil round of golf. The ground here is based on the pre 1992 back nine of the strand course and is more inland in character. The holes begin at the clubhouse and make their way down towards the River Bann.

Visitors with a little time on their hands may like to play the Riverside course to get used to the terrain and conditions before taking on the bigger challenge of the Strand Course. Holes of note include the par-4 10th (stroke index 1) and the tricky 353 yard par-4 18th.

The Old (Town) Course

The opening and closing holes of the Old Course, situated at the eastern side of Portstewart are steeped in history and tradition. Largely unchanged since the end of the 19th century, many local golfers have learnt their game on these hallowed few holes.

The 18 holes here are all made up of par-3's and par-4's. Holes 1-5 are played along the rugged shore, two of which are tricky par-3's, with the rocks ready to punish any inaccuracy off the tee.

The course crosses the road at hole 6, where a 236 yard par-3 awaits, this can be tough, especially on a on a windy day. Hole 9 (stroke index 1) is the longest hole on the course at 454 yards. The inland holes continue with six more par-4's, until you cross back over the road at hole 16 to finish out back along the shore.

Did you know? *2011 Walker Cup Hero and recently turned pro, Paul Cutler is a member of Portstewart Golf Club, his commemorative Walker Cup golf bag is proudly displayed in the club's trophy cabinet.*

Advice from the Pro!

Golf Coast Northern Ireland has a chat with Portstewart Golf Club Professional Alan Hunter.

Name: Alan Hunter

Occupation/ Position: PGA Head Professional, Portstewart Golf Club

Course Summary: Portstewart is a true links golf course with one of the finest opening holes in golf. The strand Course boasts commanding views and is sure to test every club in your bag.

My 3 tips for a visitor playing Portstewart's Strand Course for the first time:

1) As your driver will be needed on most of the Par 4's and Par 5's, the premium is on hitting the fairway, to allow any chance of making the green. Try and stay out of the thick stuff.

2) On the Causeway Coast the wind can blow extremely hard, even a strong breeze makes club selection difficult. Use a yardage book and depending on the wind and its direction don't be afraid to add a club or two up or down.

3) When facing the wind on the links, it helps to choke down on a longer, less lofted club; this will make your golf ball penetrate more. Good Luck.

Alan Hunter

AWARD WINNING
ANCHOR COMPLEX
PORTSTEWART
Tel: 028 70832003

Best Food Pub 2011
Best Visitor Tourism Pub 2011
Serving Great Food 12 - 9 Daily
Taste of Ulster Highly Recommended
20 Luxury En-Suite Bedrooms

Live Entertainment 7 Nights a Week

Mon: Live Acoustic Music Session

Tue: Krazy Davy's Karaoke Show

Wed: Mark E's Quirky Quiz Night (Free Nibbles)

Thu: Live Traditional Music Session

Fri & Sat: Live Bands from 11:00pm - 1:30am

Sun: Michael E Thomas Acoustic Sessions

Club Aura Nightclub
Thu ~ Fri ~ Sat ~ Sun
10pm - Late

www.theanchorbar.co.uk

Castlerock Golf Club
'The North Coast's Hidden Gem'

> "Castlerock is the 'hidden gem' I loved the course and its 9-hole Bann Course is among the more intriguing and audacious in the game".
> **Bob Fagan 'Golf Today Magazine'**

65 Circular Road
Castlerock
Co. Londonderry
BT51 4TJ

Tel:
+44 (0) 28 70 848314
Web:
www.castlerockgc.co.uk
Email:
info@castlerockgc.co.uk
Twitter: @CastlerockGC

Club Manager/Secretary:
Mark Steen

Club Professional:
Thomas Johnston

Course Details

Architect:
Ben Sayers & Harry Colt

Mussenden Links:
18 holes Par 73 6805 yards
(Handicap certificate required)

Course Record:
Paul McGinley 64

Bann Course:
9 holes Par 68 4892 yards

Course Type:
Links

Course Facilities:

Club History

Castlerock Golf Club was founded in 1901 after local landowners, the Bruce family gave permission to use a large part of ground for the purposes of golf. Initially there were only nine holes and the inaugural open stroke competition that took place on the 22nd June attracted interest from far and wide, first prize and the princely sum of £3 went to 5 handicapper, J Hunter-Steen from Cheltenham Golf club for a gross score of 84 (Nett 79). It was reported that the "weather turned out disagreeable for all".

The club wanted to expand and in 1906 entered into negotiations with the Dugan family to secure another tract of land on a long lease, Sir Hervey Bruce assisted this by extending the lease on his own land for a peppercorn rent. Once the land passed into the control of the club, the council commissioned Scottish club designer and manufacturer Ben Sayers to design a further nine holes. Completed and officially opened on 15th July 1909, the occasion was marked by a large gathering of ladies and gentlemen and Sir Hervey driving the first ever ball from the first tee and declaring the new 18-hole course officially open.

In 1925 the world famous golf course architect Henry Shapland "Harry" Colt, designer of neighbouring Royal Portrush Golf Club made several alterations and is largely responsible for the design of the Mussenden links as we know it today.

Intro

Castlerock is a small seaside village about five miles to the west of Coleraine; the population is around 1300 but swells in the summer months due to the large number of holiday style properties. It has a 1km long sandy beach that runs from the lower Bann Estuary (Barmouth) to the large sea cliffs at Downhill. In comparison to Portrush and Portstewart, Castlerock is a quaint little resort that offers a relaxing and laid back atmosphere. Situated along the main Londonderry to Belfast railway line, this section of the journey is renowned as being one of the most scenic in the world.

The position of Castlerock Golf Club itself couldn't be any more dramatic, set amongst rolling sand dunes with the River Bann running into the Atlantic Ocean to the north (on the opposite side of the estuary to Portstewart golf club); the views from the course are absolutely spectacular. With the Donegal headlands visible to one side, look to the north east and if you have a clear day you'll catch sight of Scotland's Westerly Isles. It is said that Castlerock is one of the purest links courses that you could find anywhere; golf was made to be played on land like this.

Having to live in the shadow of more illustrious neighbours, Castlerock offers just a supreme test of Links Golf as Royal Portrush and Portstewart. With these famous links courses in such close proximity, Castlerock is often missed out by travelling golfers, for those that do make the trip; they are often overwhelmed by just how good this course is.

"Castlerock goes all but unnoticed by visiting golfers - a tragedy for such a stunning links and an even greater tragedy for the visitors. Miss this beauty and you are missing a treat."
David Brice "Golf International Inc"

Intro (cont)

Graced with such natural beauty and being in a more peaceful setting, Castlerock has been described as a 'sacred retreat for the truly ardent follower of golf'.

Renowned for having high quality greens all year round, Paul McGinley described them in 2001 as been as good as, if not better than what they faced at 'The Open' at Royal Lytham. Castlerock's exposed location makes it very susceptible to the wind, in 2001, during the 'Irish PGA International', Paul McGinley shot a 64 on a calm day, breaking the course record in the process. On the previous day when the wind was up, eventual winner, Des Smith was the only player to break par.

Castlerock will not disappoint, the course ticks all the usual links boxes, undulating fairways, bumps and hollows, unforgiving rough and some of the finest greens you could ever wish to putt on. The Club has a well appointed clubhouse with full bar and catering facilities and is described by Golf & Incentive Travel as one of the most welcoming clubs in Ireland.

Did you know?
In his youth, Northern Ireland's European Tour star, Michael Hoey honed his golfing skills on the links at Castlerock; his parents owned a holiday house in the resort.

Courses

Mussenden Links

Regarded as one of Ireland's finest links courses the Championship Mussenden course is a par 73 with five par-5's, four par-3's and nine par-4's. As with any links course, the key here is to keep your ball in play, the rough is unforgiving. Pay particular attention to your short game too, the greens are lightning fast, even in winter time.

The Mussenden link's opening and closing holes are inland along the railway line, but the more memorable holes are in the true, links land in-between. Saying that, hole-1 is one tough cookie, a 367yrd, uphill, dogleg right with another steep rise before the green. Your second shot may require more club than you first think.

Holes 3, 4 and 5 have the railway line running down the right hand side. Hole 3, the first of the par-5's plays long at 523yds, the threat of out of bounds to the right tends to force tee shots left, too left and you'll end up in the rough. Our feature hole, Leg O Mutton (Hole-4) is a fantastic par-3 that will last long in the memory. The Par-4 seventh, known as the armchair is rated as the hardest hole on the course, with its nestled green surrounded by imposing sand hills. Hole-8, the aptly named bulldozer is another tough, uphill par-4. The outward 9 comes to an end with a 214 yard par-3, Quarry, with its small green surrounded by bumps and hollows.

After the turn, you are presented with one excellent links hole after another. The 15th is a tough par-5, named homewards and presents a blind tee shot which, if played correctly, offers a great chance to score well. Beware the strategically placed sentinel bunker. Hole 16, the short, 167yrd par-3 that rewards a well placed tee shot with a nice birdie opportunity, leads onto two great closing holes.

Hole number & name	Championship yardage	Par	Stroke Index
1 Knocklayde	367	4	9
2 Sconce	375	4	5
3 The Whins	523	5	13
4 Leg O Mutton	200	3	11
5 Railway	477	5	15
6 Burn	347	4	7
7 Armchair	418	4	1
8 Bulldozer	411	4	3
9 Quarry	214	3	17
Out	**3332**		
10 Fairy Dell	415	4	4
11 Coastguards	529	5	16
12 Spion Kop	430	4	2
13 Swallow Hill	382	4	14
14 Corner	192	3	8
15 Homewards	518	5	6
16 Summit	157	3	18
17 Inishowen	493	5	12
18 Mussenden	357	4	10
In	**3473**		
Out	**3332**		
Total	**6805**		

Before you tackle Hole 17, a tricky 493yrd par-5 with its long narrow fairway, take a moment to savour the view from the tee. The par-4 18th (Mussenden) is a dog-leg right with an elevated, two tiered green, a difficult closing hole that offers a fitting end to such a wonderful test of true links golf.

Courses
Bann Course

The 9-hole Bann course has been described as being among the more intriguing and audacious in the game. Set out completely in the dunes closest to the sea, the scenery here is simply stunning. Added in the 1980's and based on a Frank Pennink design, the Bann Course is located beyond the caravan park, behind the club house.

Once on the course you feel almost cocooned, isolated in a golfing wonderland. This is links golf in its purest form and it's hard to even notice the fact that there are no bunkers; the terrain here offers enough of a hazard. The 491yd par-5 5th, 'Bannview' would be a worthy addition to any golf club in the land. Played downhill, with the River Bann meandering to your right, the green is protected by sand hills on the other three sides; the spectacular views of the river heading out towards the mighty Atlantic Ocean are stunning.

Interesting Facts:

* On his visit to Castlerock in 2003 Oscar winning actor Michael Douglas described the course as pure heaven.

* The Par 5 5th on the Bann Course is considered to be one of the most scenic holes in Irish Golf.

* Castlerock Golf Club is twinned with Niagara Golf Club, North America's oldest Golf course.

Featured Hole :
4th Hole "Leg o' Mutton" *(Mussenden course)*

So named because of its unique shape, the 200 yard par-3 has a railway line to the right, a burn to the left and the tee shot has to be played on to a raised green. A challenging hole that when negotiated successfully will provide a huge sigh of relief.

> *"The Leg of Mutton, one of the single most talked about golf challenges in Northern Ireland golfing circles"*
> **John Redmond "Great Golf Courses of Ireland"**

Famous Visitors:
- Actor & star of Wall Street Michael Douglas
- 1987 US Open Winner Scott Simpson

Advice from the Pro!

Golf Coast Northern Ireland has a chat with Castlerock Golf Club Professional Thomas Johnston.

Name: Thomas Johnston

Occupation/ Position: PGA Head Professional, Castlerock Golf Club

Course Summary: Castlerock Golf Club is a tough but fair links course. Golfers visiting for the first time can sometimes be surprised by just how much the wind blows here, so keeping the ball in play is a must.

My 3 tips for a visitor playing Castlerock for the first time:

1) Think carefully about what club to use off the tee, sometimes a 3 wood/rescue or even an iron is a better play to set you up for the approach shot. Try and use the wind, but don't fight it and never force a golf shot into it, take plenty of club and swing smoothly with a three quarter swing, you will be surprised by the results.

2) Use a stroke-saver, GPS system or a caddie to get the most out of your round. Even something simple like avoiding one of the many bunkers at Castlerock could turn an average round into a memorable one. Remember, the more knowledge you have about each hole, the better. Tiger Woods based his entire game plan around not finding bunkers in the 2006 Open at Liverpool. It worked.

3) Have a good warm up on the putting green and chipping area. The excellent greens at Castlerock are usually running fast, even in winter time and can catch a lot of people out with their speed. A good way to practice on the putting green is to stand somewhere on the green and try to roll the ball just onto the fringe. This helps to quickly build up your feel for the speed of the greens and the practice putting green is usually the same pace as the ones on the golf course.

Thomas Johnston

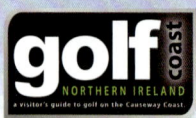

Ballycastle Golf Club
'A unique mix of pure, unadulterated links with five opening parkland holes thrown in for good measure.'

"The first five parkland holes are flanked by two rivers and the ruins of a 12th Century Abbey, then it's pure links golf packed with variety and the distraction of picture postcard sea views all the way to the clubhouse".
David Brice Golf International inc

2 Cushendall Road
Ballycastle
Co. Antrim
BT54 6QP
Tel: +44 (0)28 2076 2536

Web:
www.ballycastlegolfclub.com

Email:
info@ballycastlegolfclub.com

Twitter:
@BallycastleGC

Club Manager/Secretary:
Trevor Peacock

Club Professional:
Damian McEvoy

Course Details

Architect:
Commander Alfred Malcolm Causton R.N.

Course:
18 holes Par 71 5876 yards

Course Record:
64 Mark McCormick

Course Type:
Links/Parkland

Club History

According to the club's archives, it was generally believed that Ballycastle Golf Club was founded in 1891. The club began preparing for their centenary in the mid 1980's and appointed a centenary committee so they could celebrate this milestone in fine style.

However, in 1986 a letter landed at the club house from a Mr Brian Page from East Sussex, England. He had unearthed a putter with the following inscription: "Presented to Commander A .M. Causton R.N. by the members of the Ballycastle Golf Club at a complimentary dinner given to him on 8th August 1894 in recognition of his indefatigable exertions in forming the club in 1890 and acting as its Honorary Secretary ever since". The club's centenary plans were up in the air, would they have to celebrate a year earlier?

It was decided that the appearance of this presentation putter was the strongest available proof that the club was indeed, founded in 1890 and not 1891, as was largely thought. The centenary celebrations were brought forward to 1990. It was accepted that whilst the formalities of the club were incepted in 1891, it was probably in 1890 that the planning and clearing of an area of dune land known as the Warren was first undertaken. Commander Alfred Malcolm Causton retired from the navy in 1880 and joined the Coastguard service; he was posted to Ballycastle as an inspecting officer in 1882.

Having first played golf at the County Club in Portrush, he noticed that the land at the Warren in Ballycastle would be an ideal area for locals to take up the game. The land at the Warren was owned by a Miss Kathleen Boyd whose family controlled large swathes of land throughout North Antrim for centuries. Miss Boyd was a keen golfer and had no hesitation in allowing Commander Causton to formally lay out the course on her land; in fact she was so keen that she offered the land at the Warren rent free for a period of twenty years. This allowed the club to thrive and Miss Boyd continued to subsidise the club right throughout its formative years, her generosity was acknowledged in 1897, when she was elected the club's first ever Lady Captain, a position she held until 1944.

> *Did you know?* Ballycastle Golf Club is one of the founding members of the Golfing Union of Ireland (GUI), the governing body of men's golf throughout Ireland. Formed in 1891, it is the oldest golfing union in the world.

Like most clubs in the area, the course was originally nine holes. Commander Causton was responsible for the design of the holes and was secretary of the club from its formal inauguration in 1891 until 1899. It's widely accepted that Commander Causton was the forefather of golf in Ballycastle and it was his foresight that inspired the formation of Ballycastle Golf Club. Despite returning to England in the early part of the century, he continued to be captain of the club from 1903, until his death in 1921.

Putting at the Glenshesk hole in the 1890's, the figure holding the flag is club founder Commander A M Causton. **Picture courtesy of Ballycastle Golf Club.**

In 1906, with membership growing, it was found that the course had become inadequate for its members. Successful negotiations with Miss Boyd's representatives had helped to secure some further lands for the club. The original nine holes were converted to six and the new land was used to construct three brand new holes, this increased the yardage from 1926yds to 2680yds. A new club house was constructed in 1901 and although now fully rebuilt, it remains in the same location as the original.

> *Did you know?* The prominent Irish Nationalist, Sir Roger Casement, who was tried and hung for treason by Britain in 1916 was a member of Ballycastle Golf Club and served as captain in 1921/22. According to minutes, he was acting captain for a number of years previous to this, when club founder, Commander Causton resided in England.

It wasn't until 1926, that the next alterations were made to the course. A parcel of land on the opposite side of the Cushendall Road next to the Margy and Carey rivers was secured and a brand new opening five holes were constructed. The new layout was officially opened by the Governor of Northern Ireland, The Duke of Abercorn on the 17th August 1926. The course has remained largely unchanged since then.

Bonamargy Abbey

Not many golf courses can boast a 12th Century Abbey, housing the remains of an ancient Irish Chieftain as an out of bounds. Ballycastle's third hole is flanked by the ruins of Bonamargy (meaning foot of the River Margy) Abbey.

Bonamargy was established by Rory McQuillan, the McQuillans came from Scotland with a small army in the 1460's and laid claim on lands around North Antrim; they became tenants of Dunluce Castle until they were ousted by the rival MacDonnell clan.

The remains of an altar can still be found in the Church adjoining the Abbey and the locked vaults contain the remains of Sorley Boy MacDonnell, a celebrated Irish Chieftain. Sorley Boy was the son of Alexander MacDonnell, the Lord of Islay and Kintyre. He was born at Dunanynie Castle near Ballycastle and helped repel Shane O'Neil, who tried to oust the clan and reclaim their lands for the English Crown.

The most famous resident of the Abbey was the 17th Century prophet and recluse, Julie MacQuillen. Known as the 'Black Nun', MacQuillen wished to be buried at the entrance to the chapel so she would be trodden on as people entered. A Celtic cross marks her grave at the western end of the main Church. Her Ghost is said to haunt the Abbey.

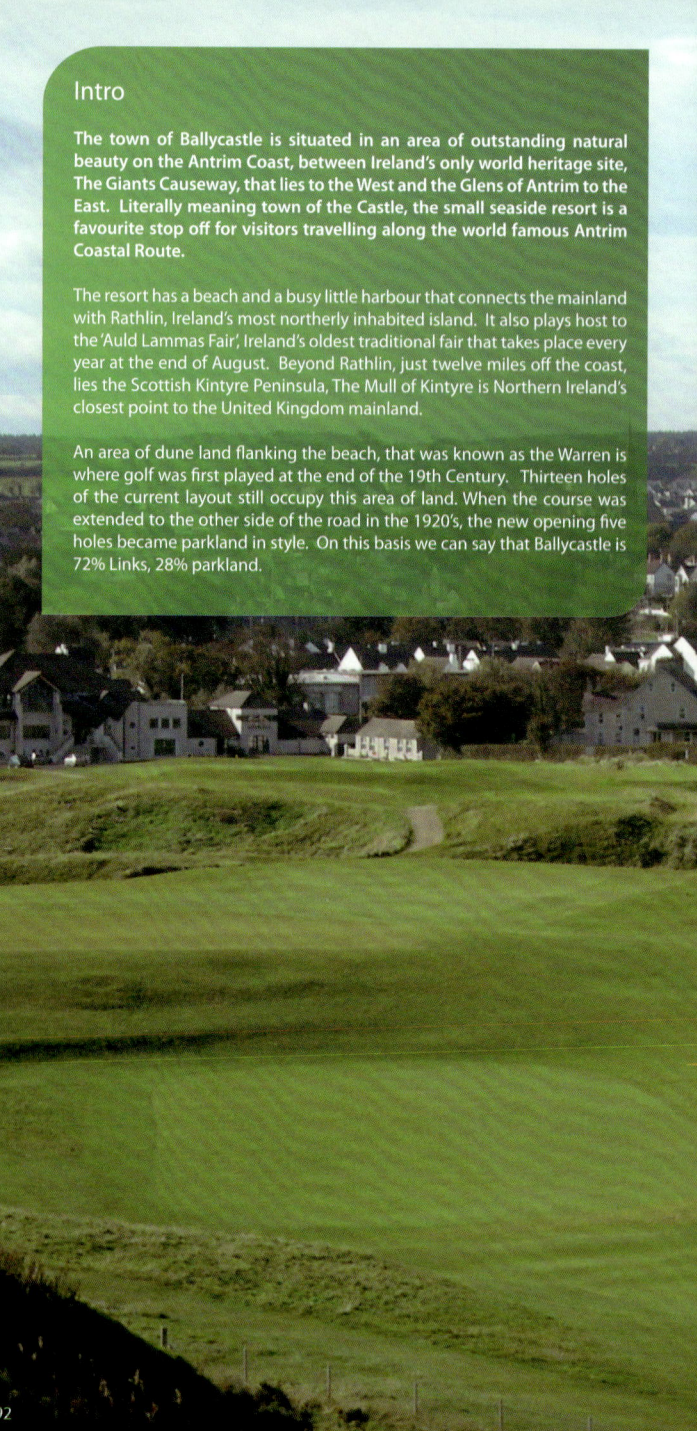

Intro

The town of Ballycastle is situated in an area of outstanding natural beauty on the Antrim Coast, between Ireland's only world heritage site, The Giants Causeway, that lies to the West and the Glens of Antrim to the East. Literally meaning town of the Castle, the small seaside resort is a favourite stop off for visitors travelling along the world famous Antrim Coastal Route.

The resort has a beach and a busy little harbour that connects the mainland with Rathlin, Ireland's most northerly inhabited island. It also plays host to the 'Auld Lammas Fair', Ireland's oldest traditional fair that takes place every year at the end of August. Beyond Rathlin, just twelve miles off the coast, lies the Scottish Kintyre Peninsula, The Mull of Kintyre is Northern Ireland's closest point to the United Kingdom mainland.

An area of dune land flanking the beach, that was known as the Warren is where golf was first played at the end of the 19th Century. Thirteen holes of the current layout still occupy this area of land. When the course was extended to the other side of the road in the 1920's, the new opening five holes became parkland in style. On this basis we can say that Ballycastle is 72% Links, 28% parkland.

Described by 'top 100 Golf courses' as a quirky little course, with many changes of elevation, Ballycastle is one of those courses that will leave an indelible impression on all who visit. The links land that occupies holes 6 -18 is the finest of golfing terrain that requires extremely accurate iron play; the undulating greens will test your putting skills to the max. Holes 11-17 run up one side of a cliff, along the top, then down the other side.

The opening five parkland holes run alongside the River Margy, with the ruins of Bonamargy Abbey providing an interesting hazard. Once you cross onto the links, you are treated with some of the finest views from a golf course anywhere in Ireland. The 'top holes' offer panoramic views of Rathlin Island, The Mull of Kintyre, The North Antrim Coastline, Glenshesk and the hills of Donegal.

Ballycastle is renowned for its warm hospitality, the friendliness of its members and the overall welcoming atmosphere. A new modern clubhouse was constructed in 2003 and provides excellent bar and catering facilities with magnificent views over the course.

The Courses
The Course

The Opening parkland holes begin with a long par-5 that curves its way along the banks of the Margy river, a long drive will leave the green in range, but with the river to the right, and trees and three fairway bunkers to the left, accuracy is the key, a lay-up shot may be your best answer here.

Hole 2, Gleshesk (stroke index 3) has an elevated tee and offers a superb view along the fairway to Bonamargy Abbey. This dogleg right requires an accurate second shot to a green that is well guarded by bunkers. The par-3 3rd has danger both left and right, and runs alongside the graveyard of Bonamargy Abbey; once again, accuracy is the key here. Hole 4, rated the hardest on the course, is a long par-4 that tees off next to the roadside and is played back towards the banks of the River Carey, the green is protected by two front bunkers.

Hole number & name	Championship yardage	Par	Stroke Index
1 The Margy	456	5	9
2 Glenshesk	351	4	3
3 The Abbey	166	3	13
4 Carey	408	4	1
5 Dunrainie	259	4	17
6 Hog's Back	319	4	15
7 The Beach	404	4	7
8 Knocklayde	327	4	11
9 The Dooans	353	4	5
Out	3043		
10 The Chasm	115	3	12
11 Rathlin	347	4	4
12 Fairhead	489	5	14
13 Vincey's Pitch	146	3	16
14 Tim's Corner	355	4	2
15 Kinbane	402	4	8
16 Culfeightrin	294	4	18
17 The Pitch	183	3	6
18 Dalriada	502	5	10
In	2833		
Out	3043		
Total	5876		

The links section of the course begins at the 6th, a 319yd par-4 that runs alongside Ballycastle Beach; this is the point on the course where wind speed and direction comes into play. Even a small breeze coming off the ocean should have a bearing on your club selection here.

Take a moment to savour the views from the 7th Tee. The slight dogleg left requires an accurate tee shot, that if struck well, will leave a shortish 2nd shot to a basin shaped green that is protected by a cross bunker approximately 20yds short. The 9th, listed by the Irish Independent as the best hole of its number in Ireland, requires an iron off the tee to leave a short uphill approach to an elevated green, inaccuracy here will be severely punished.

Another hole that requires accuracy off the tee is the par-3 10th, the shortest hole on the course at 115yds. This blind tee shot has to be played over a chasm, which is guarded by an out of bounds to the left and deep sloping rough on the approach, the exposed, elevated green undulates in several directions, so setting down onto it can be tricky and that's on a calm day.

> ***Did you Know!*** *"The spectacular cliff visible from the 7th tee is known as Fairhead and is Northern Ireland's most Northerly point. It is said, that if The Mull of Kintyre is visible in the distance it will soon rain, if it is not visible, it is already raining.*

The 13th green is the furthest point from the clubhouse, the homewards journey begins at the 14th, a tricky par-4 (stroke index 2), the fairway slopes left to right and the green is guarded by a bunker front and right.

The 16th is one of those holes that can both reward and punish, this short dogleg par-4 has numerous tiny bunkers protecting the small green, an accurate iron shot to the right off the tee will open up the green, leaving a straightforward approach.

After the featured 17th the 18th is a fine closing par-5, keep your tee shot right to avoid the out of bounds to the left, the green's close proximity to the car park and the panoramic viewing windows of the clubhouse can intimidate many a golfer.

Course Map

Did you know? *When first established in 1890, Ballycastle Golf Club was known as the 'Warren Links', in reference to the stretch of sandy turf that the opening nine holes were laid out on.*

Featured Hole:
17th 'The Pitch'

The views from the 17th, the last of the 'top holes' are amongst the best on the course, but rest assured, this hole isn't just renowned for its exhilarating view. A memorable par-3 is always recalled by a visiting golfer. They don't get much more memorable than this. The elevated tee, set right on the cliff edge requires a straight iron shot to the green, 183 yards away. The green is actually 100 feet below the tee and is protected by 6 bunkers, both short of and along each side. A tiered green can result in a tricky putt for par. A three on this hole should be viewed as a possibility, rather than a certainty.

> ***What they say?*** *Ballycastle is a 'thinker's course 'and this is no more evident than at the par-3 17th – also known as 'The Pitch' – where the golfer must play to a green some 100 feet below the level of the tee.*
> *Yourgolftravel.com*

Bunkers!

For those golfers who are unfortunate enough to end up in one of the many new bunkers dotted along the opening five holes at Ballycastle, you can lay the blame firmly, with one of the Causeway Coast's most famous golfing sons.

When Godfrey Clarke was course manager at Ballycastle, he asked his son Darren to take a look at the bunkering and perhaps suggest something new to 'freshen' things up.

As Captain at the time, Brian Dillan recalls how the trio drove around in a buggy and sought Darren's advice, "the idea for the new bunkering was completely Darren's", he adds. "We got free advice from Northern Ireland's top golfer, but we entertained him afterwards with the black stuff!" The Club thanked Darren Clarke properly in 2000 after his defeat of Tiger Woods in the World Championship Match Play event and made him an honorary member of Ballycastle Golf Club. Perhaps this was Darren Clarke's first foray into Golf Course Design?

Advice from the Pro!

Golf Coast Northern Ireland has a chat with Ballycastle Golf Club Professional Damien McEvoy.

Name: Damien McEvoy

Occupation/ Position: PGA Head Professional, Ballycastle Golf Club

Course Summary: Ballycastle offers a challenging but enjoyable test of golf. Accurate iron play is essential for a good score, while undulating greens will test your putting skills to their maximum. The course is unique, in that it offers both a diverse parkland layout in its opening 5 holes and then true seaside links in the remaining thirteen holes.

My 3 tips for a visitor playing Ballycastle Golf Course for the first time:

1) Course management is important at Ballycastle. There are many blind shots, beware of the Margy River, the beach and the gorse bushes. Distance is not the key here, but accuracy is. A driver is not always the preferred club. The 10th hole is a famous par 3 that offers a blind tee shot, always take more club than you think and don't be left or long!

2) Before you play Ballycastle, practise your low stinger shots. The golfer with a high ball fight will end up on the beach. The lob shot may look impressive, but here at Ballycastle, the ' bump and run' is the shot to have in the bag.

3) My last piece of advice is to leave plenty of time to have a look around the well stocked Professional shop; there are many products with all the top brands well represented. We have a great range of crested sweaters, Polo Tops and other items to remind you of your trip to Ballycastle.

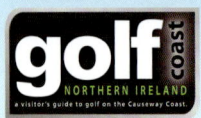

Gracehill Golf Club

'American style greens & water hazards provide an interesting contrast to the Coast's links jewels.'

> "The incorporation of so many water features may not sit comfortably with golfing purists, but there's no denying this American design influence has had everything to do with making this a very challenging, contemporary course"
> *Top100golfcourses.com*

141 Ballinlea Road
Stranocum
Ballymoney
Co. Antrim
BT53 8PX

Tel: +44 (0) 28 20 751209

Web:
www.gracehillgolfclub.co.uk

Email:
info@gracehillgolfclub.co.uk

Twitter:
@Gracehillgc

Club Manager/Secretary:
Margaret McClure

Club Professional:
Ian Blair

Course Details

Architect:
Frank Ainsworth

Course:
18 holes Par 72 6574 yards

Course Type:
Parkland

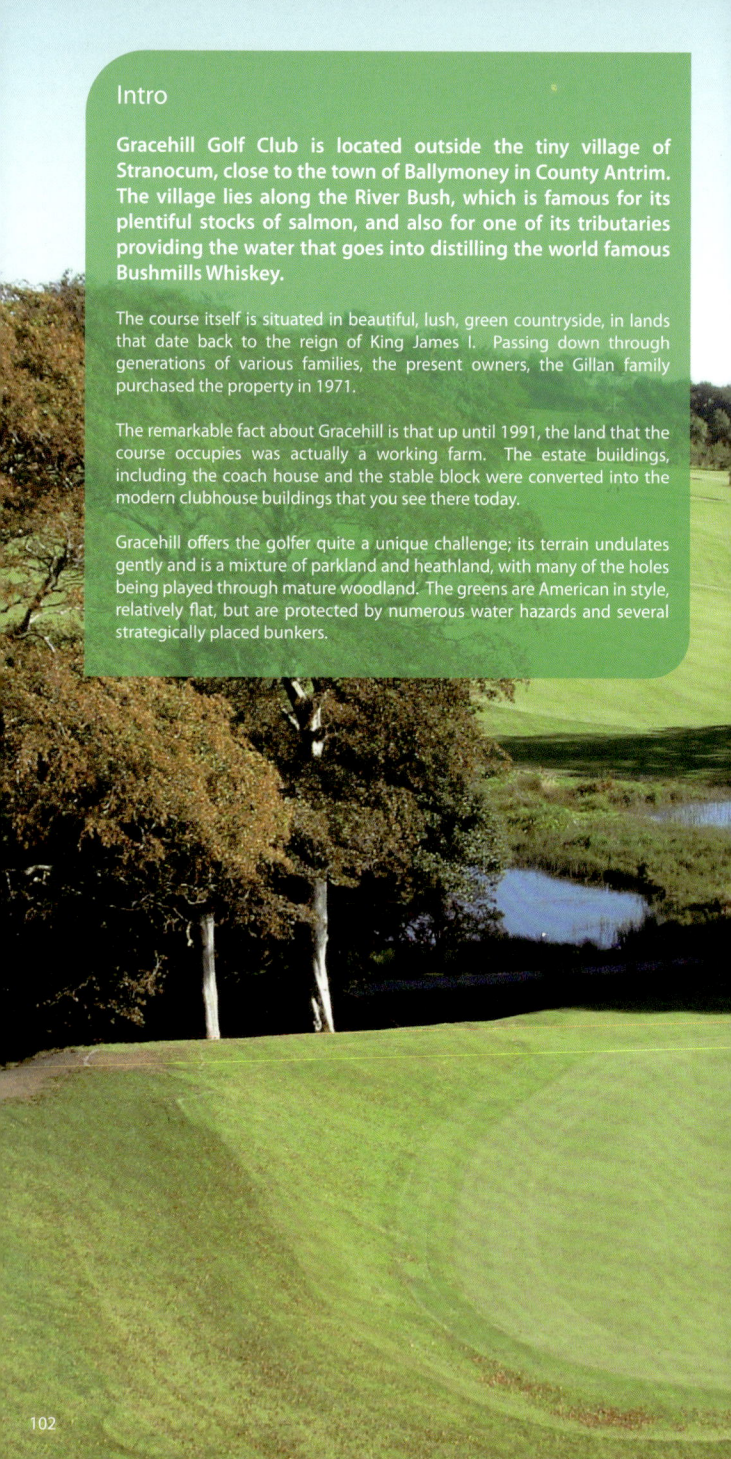

Intro

Gracehill Golf Club is located outside the tiny village of Stranocum, close to the town of Ballymoney in County Antrim. The village lies along the River Bush, which is famous for its plentiful stocks of salmon, and also for one of its tributaries providing the water that goes into distilling the world famous Bushmills Whiskey.

The course itself is situated in beautiful, lush, green countryside, in lands that date back to the reign of King James I. Passing down through generations of various families, the present owners, the Gillan family purchased the property in 1971.

The remarkable fact about Gracehill is that up until 1991, the land that the course occupies was actually a working farm. The estate buildings, including the coach house and the stable block were converted into the modern clubhouse buildings that you see there today.

Gracehill offers the golfer quite a unique challenge; its terrain undulates gently and is a mixture of parkland and heathland, with many of the holes being played through mature woodland. The greens are American in style, relatively flat, but are protected by numerous water hazards and several strategically placed bunkers.

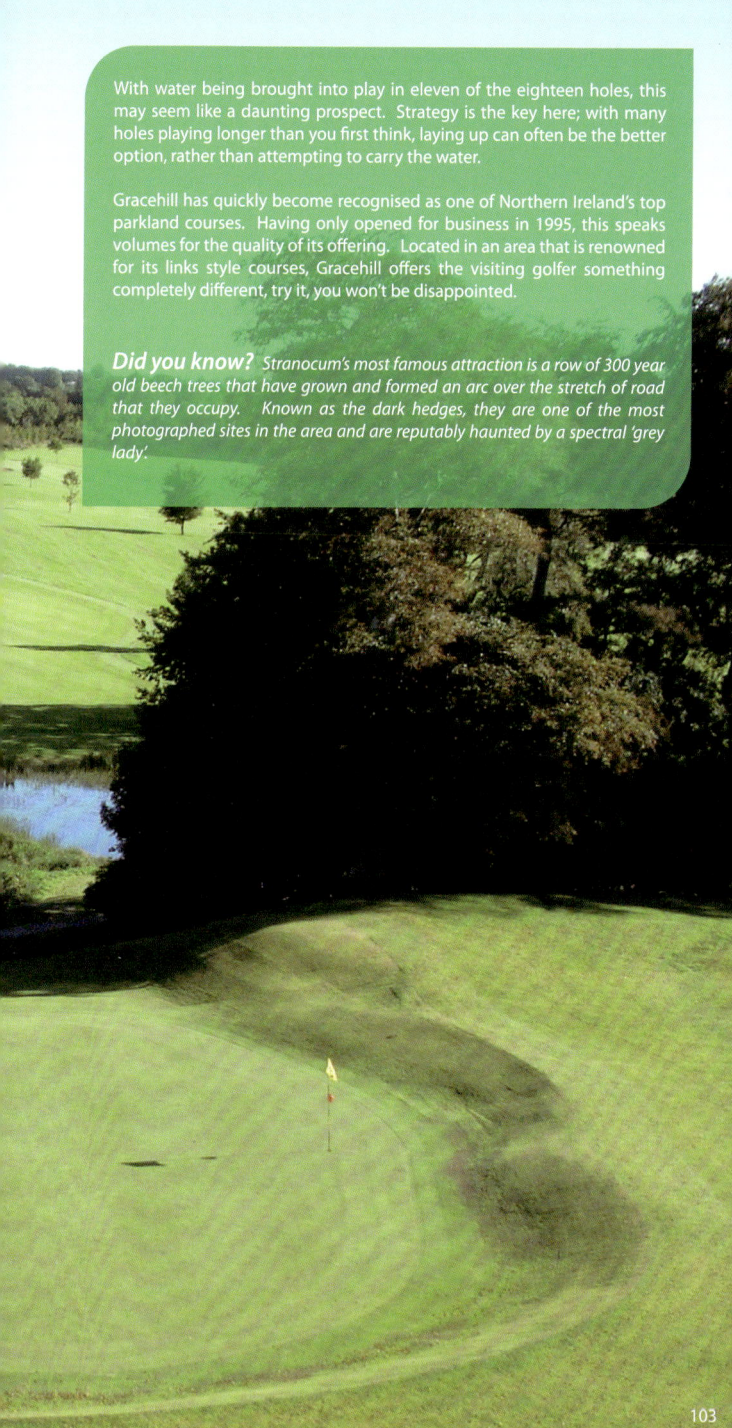

With water being brought into play in eleven of the eighteen holes, this may seem like a daunting prospect. Strategy is the key here; with many holes playing longer than you first think, laying up can often be the better option, rather than attempting to carry the water.

Gracehill has quickly become recognised as one of Northern Ireland's top parkland courses. Having only opened for business in 1995, this speaks volumes for the quality of its offering. Located in an area that is renowned for its links style courses, Gracehill offers the visiting golfer something completely different, try it, you won't be disappointed.

Did you know? Stranocum's most famous attraction is a row of 300 year old beech trees that have grown and formed an arc over the stretch of road that they occupy. Known as the dark hedges, they are one of the most photographed sites in the area and are reputably haunted by a spectral 'grey lady'.

The Course

If you're looking for a gentle introduction at Gracehill, forget it, the opening par 4, 'Crow's Nest' requires you to be on top of your game from the off. After such a dramatic opening hole you can breathe easy until the water comes back into play at hole-5, this is a long par-4 at 448 yards, be careful not to over club on your second shot as you'll end up in the pond beyond the green. Water, in one guise or another is almost a constant feature from here on in, with it being such a hazard, accuracy from the tee is a necessity.

Hole number & name	Championship yardage	Par	Stroke Index
1 Crow's Nest	344	4	10
2 Calhame	348	4	18
3 The Knowe	378	4	16
4 Frank's	492	5	6
5 Iderdown	448	4	2
6 Serenity	374	4	14
7 McCool's Quarry	183	3	8
8 Keyhole	386	4	4
9 The Willows	486	5	12
Out	3439		
10 Doughery Burn	478	4	3
11 Fuschia Island	163	3	13
12 Sycamore	487	5	7
13 Knockmore	415	4	1
14 Wing 'n a Prayer	211	3	5
15 Amen	471	5	11
16 Oasis	146	3	15
17 Silver Birch	359	4	17
18 Yew Turn	405	4	9
In	3135		
Out	3439		
Total	6574		

What they say? Hole 1- A decent opening drive will leave you with around 170-yards of pond to carry off a downhill lie into a raised green, barely visible through a tunnel of trees. Get the ball in the air and pray.
Stuart Hood Golf World Magazine

Hole 10 is another tough par-4 at 478yds (stroke index 3), where your second shot is played to a green protected by a large pond to the left. After the featured 11th hole, holes 13, 14 and 15 are all worth a mention.

The par-4 13th, Knockmore is the hardest hole on the course and is a card-maker or breaker. Big hitters may try to take out the slight dog leg, but with trees and laurels running the entire length of the hole, this may be a risky option. A strategic tee shot, finding the middle of the fairway is a safer bet here.

Hole 14, the aptly named 'Wing 'n a Prayer' could be one of the toughest par-3's in Ireland and requires a tee shot to be played over yet another pond, to a green with a central elevated spine running along its length.

> **Did you Know!** Darren Clarke has played Gracehill on numerous occasions; his favourite hole is the toughest on the course, the par-4 13th.

The par-5 15th known as 'Amen' has an 'S' shaped fairway. With a direct line you are presented with the opportunity to turn this into a long par-4, but don't take the birdie for granted, with out of bounds to the left and trees to the right, you must be super-accurate off the tee.

The closing hole requires a drive over water once again, and has a slight dog-leg to the right. With out of bounds to the left, to find the centre of the fairway, your tee shot requires both length and accuracy, this will leave an uphill approach to a green protected by mature trees and a strategically placed bunker to the right.

Featured Hole:
11th 'Fuschia Island'

Holes with island greens are amongst the most spectacular in the world, the 17th of the Stadium Course at TPC Sawgrass is probably the most famous. The Causeway Coast has its very own island green with the 11th at Gracehill, 'Fuschia Island'. This 163yrd par-3 (stroke index 13) is surrounded by water on all sides.

With water being such a feature for the majority of holes at Gracehill, it only comes into play for the poorest of shots. That's not the case for the 11th though, bailing out is definitely not an option here, an accurate drive 160yds to the centre of the green, leaving two putts for par will do nicely.

Advice from the Pro!

Golf Coast Northern Ireland has a chat with Gracehill Golf Club Professional Ian Blair.

Name: Ian Blair

Occupation/ Position: PGA Director of Golf, Gracehill Golf Club

Course Summary: Having only been 16 years in existence, Gracehill has already established itself as probably the most challenging parkland course within easy reach of the Causeway Coast. With plenty of water and mature trees, Gracehill can prove a test for golfers with all levels of ability.

My **3** tips for a visitor playing Gracehill Golf Course for the first time:

1) Accuracy is the name of the game at Gracehill. If you're not in the correct position with your approach play, take your punishment, lay-up if required and don't try the 'Hail Mary' shot.

2) Try to build your round slowly. Besides the first hole, which features two water hazards and a raised green that is positioned between two rows of mighty beech trees, the first few holes allow you to get yourself warmed up and into your stride. From the sixth hole onwards, this 'easy' start is quickly forgotten with water featuring on the next seven holes.

3) Unlike the links courses on the Causeway Coast, at Gracehill there is very little 'bounce and roll', you must play the yardage to the flag and attack the hole. 2010 US Open Champion, Graeme McDowell likes to practice here, as the course requires you knowing how far your ball will travel through the air to the hole and not how far the ball will 'run out'. Play 'front of green' golf at your peril here, as it will bring the water hazards into play.

Ian Blair

golf coast NORTHERN IRELAND
a visitor's guide to golf on the Causeway Coast.

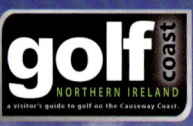

Roe Park Golf Resort

'Superb Parkland golf in the historic setting of the Roe Park Estate'.

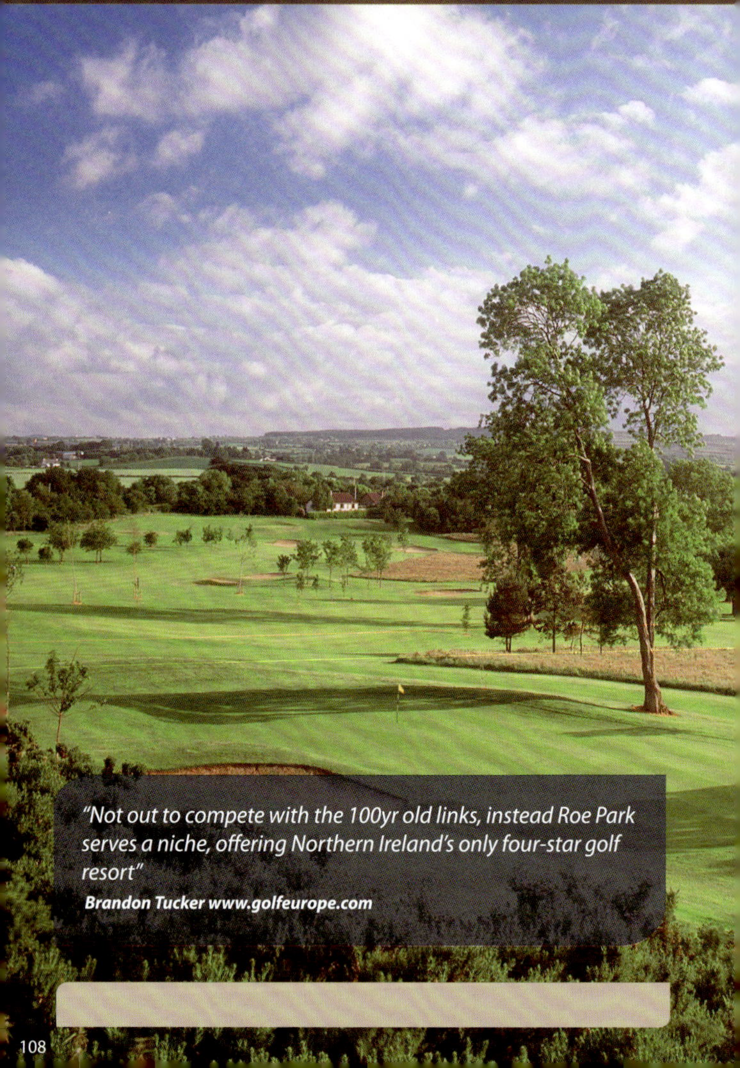

"Not out to compete with the 100yr old links, instead Roe Park serves a niche, offering Northern Ireland's only four-star golf resort"

Brandon Tucker www.golfeurope.com

Drumrane Road
Limavady
Co. Londonderry
BT49 9LB

Tel: +44 (0) 28 77 722222

Web:
www.roeparkresort.com

Email:
terry.kelly@roeparkresort.com

Twitter:
@RoeParkResort

Club Manager/Secretary:
Terry Kelly

Club Professional:
Shaun Devenny

Course Details

Architect:
Frank Ainsworth

Course:
18 holes Par 70 6322 yards

Course Type:
Parkland

Intro

Roe Park Golf Resort is located at the edge of the thriving Co. Londonderry market town of Limavady. Set in the picturesque Roe Valley, under the shadows of the mighty Binevenagh Mountain, the golf resort occupies lands adjacent to the famous Roe Valley Country Park.

The park runs three miles along the banks of the River Roe and boasts some of the finest open forest and woodland areas in Northern Ireland. These provide a stunning backdrop as the Roe twists turns and plunges through some spectacular gorges and ravines.

Roe Park cannot be described as a typical resort course with broad fairways and massive greens; it's much more than that. Course designer, Frank Ainsworth has skilfully sculpted the layout to blend in with the splendid surroundings and this is the reason that Roe Park is now rated as one of the best parkland courses in Northern Ireland. Inland courses aren't usually renowned for their vistas, but Roe Park's location at the edge of the Sperrin Mountains, with Eagle Rock to the North and Donegal's Inishowen Peninsula to the West, provides a magnificent setting.

The resort occupies some 155 acres and the course is laid out on lands that have played a significant part in the history of Ireland. St Columba, the patron saint of Derry was said to have returned here from Iona to attend the convention of Drumcreat, where famously, all the bards and chieftains of Ireland met in 575AD to discuss the matters of the day.

With the River Roe twisting its way around the lower part of the course, the upper holes are centred around Mullagh Hill. The River and several lakes provide challenging water features.

Located in an area that is renowned for its links courses, Roe Park pitches itself quite cleverly, not competing with, but offering superb facilities in the hope of complimenting these famous tracks. Roe Park Resort is within easy driving distance to all of the Causeway's Coast's top courses. The resort boasts a golf academy, an outdoor, floodlit driving range, an indoor driving range and an interactive video coaching system. There is a well stocked pro shop, a short game practice area and a putting green.

The award winning four-star hotel and spa offers all the usual facilities and the Coach House restaurant, located above the pro shop has large viewing windows offering superb views over the course.

Did you know? J.E. Ritter who had a house in Roe Park developed the first ever hydo-electric power station in Northern Ireland. His invention still stands in the Park and as a tribute; the first hole at Roe Park is named in his honour

The Course

Ever since Roe Park was conceived in the early 90's the club, its facilities and the course itself have constantly evolved and improved. The latest changes to the course took place in 2010 and were undertaken by the famous golf course architects, Hawtree Ltd.

The course at Roe Park has two distinct sections, the opening five holes, known as the 'lower five' are situated close to the River Roe with the long par-5 2nd and the par-5 4th actually running alongside the river.

If you wish to score well here, you'll require a lightning start, birdie opportunities come along early on holes 2 and 4. On 4, watch your approach shot to the green, the river will punish anything left or long.

The long par-3 3rd, 'Betty Annes', stuck neatly between the two par-5's is the first tough hole. At 210yds from the back tee, it requires a well hit shot over two lakes that are situated to the front and left of the green, be content with your par here.

With its close proximity to the river, the land that occupies the lower five can get quite wet in winter, so beware when putting as the greens can be quite spongy off-season.

Eleven of the remaining thirteen holes are built around the historic Mullagh Hill, where a number of lakes provide the hazard. The current 9th & 10th were newly constructed in 2010 and occupy a piece of land on the opposite side of the road that leads to the hotel and clubhouse.

What they say? *"This golf course is an outstanding feature of Roe Park Resort; the 18-hole parkland layout takes full advantage of its stunning setting, with Lough Foyle and the Inishowen Peninsula providing a dramatic backdrop"*
Golf World Magazine

Hole number & name	Championship yardage	Par	Stroke Index
1 Ritters	409	4	8
2 Dogleap	560	5	12
3 Betty Annes	210	3	10
4 Roe Mill	463	5	14
5 McKeevers	394	4	2
6 Drumceatt	139	3	18
7 Slate Row	391	4	6
8 O'Cahans	398	4	4
9 Ballymore	349	4	13
Out	3313		
10 Largywood	353	4	15
11 Wiltons	160	3	16
12 Daisyhill	420	4	3
13 Mullagh	340	4	7
14 Columbas	165	3	17
15 Conns	414	4	1
16 Deer Park	498	5	9
17 Benevenagh	234	3	11
18 Roe Park	425	4	5
In	3009		
Out	3313		
Total	6322		

Holes 6-9 were all re-designed by Hawtree with the old 9th been turned into a superb par-3 (now the 11th). Hole-14, 'Columbas' is another interesting par-3 with water again being brought into play. At first glance, on this upper section the rough looks pretty tepid, but it's anything but.

After the featured 15th, you are presented with the 498yd par-5 dogleg 16th, followed by 17, a longish par-3 at 234yds and ending with 'Roe Park' a tough par-4 (stroke index 5), that can often present a tricky finish to what will have been a splendid round of golf.

Featured Hole:
15th 'Conns'

This seems to be everybody's favourite at Roe Park, described as a classic 'risk and reward' hole, the 15th is rated the hardest hole on the course. The 414yrd par-4 takes a slight dog leg right. Your tee shot from the newly designed elevated tee must find the left of the fairway to leave an approach to a green that's protected by a lake. Three bunkers, strategically placed to guard the green simply add to the fun! Any inaccuracy here will be severely punished. The 15th is a testing hole that offers a challenge to golfers of all abilities.

Advice from the Pro!

Golf Coast Northern Ireland has a chat with Roe Park Golf Club Professional Shaun Devenney.

Name: Shaun Devenney

Occupation/ Position: PGA Director of Golf, Gracehill Golf Club

Course Summary: Roe Park is a parkland course that takes full advantage of its beautiful setting with Lough Foyle and the Innishowen Peninsula providing a dramatic backdrop. Popular with amateurs and seasoned players alike, the course is both challenging and enjoyable. It is not a long course when compared to today's championship layouts, but small targets and sloping greens put an emphasis on accurate approach play.

My **3** tips for a visitor playing Roe Park for the first time:

1) With excellent facilities on site, warm up! Hit a couple of baskets of balls on the indoor range or use the fully equipped gym and get your body ready for the challenge ahead. Getting off to a good start at Roe Park is vital, there are a couple of birdie opportunities in the opening five holes; ensure that you're ready to take advantage of these.

2) With the exception of holes 8 and 15 you should favour the right hand side of the fairway when teeing off. Out of bounds and hazards come into play on the left hand side for at least ten holes of your round, this will favour those who tend to fade or slice their shots.

3) Length is not a requirement for scoring at Roe Park, but small greens and steep slopes put an emphasis on your approach shots to the greens. Accuracy and smart iron play from the fairway will help you get the most from your round. Try and leave your approach shot below the hole, and remember sometimes it's better to leave yourself a straight 10ft uphill putt than a slippery 2ft downhill putt with a severe swing. Enjoy your round.

Shaun Devenney

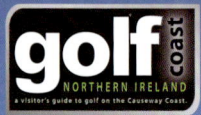

Bushfoot Golf Club
'A fantastic little links course set in an area of outstanding natural beauty'.

50 Bushfoot Road
Portballintrae
Bushmills
Co. Antrim
BT57 8RR

Tel: +44 (0) 28 2073 1317

Web:
www.bushfootgolfclub.co.uk

Email:
admin@bushfootgolfclub.co.uk

Club Manager/Professional:
David Jones

Course Details

Course:
9 holes Par 70 6001 yards

Course Type:
Primarily Links with some
Park-land elements

Intro

Portballintrae is a quaint little harbour village located between the Giant's Causeway and Dunluce Castle. The village is set around a horseshoe shaped bay, where the River Bush runs into the Atlantic Ocean. Popular as a location for holiday homes, the village has grown somewhat since the first whitewashed cottages were developed close to the harbour.

The village was made famous in the late 1960's when a team of Belgian divers led by Robert Stenuit discovered the wreck of the Girona, a Galleass from the Spanish Armada that foundered off Lacada Point, near Dunluce Castle in October 1588. The gold jewellery and precious treasures that were retrieved from the wreck were brought ashore at Portballintrae and can be found on display at the Ulster Museum in Belfast.

There is a lovely golden beach known as Blackrock Strand and some fine dune-land that leads up towards the golf course. Taking its name from its location at the foot of the River Bush, Bushfoot Golf Club can trace its origins back to 1890, but it is believed that golf was played on the lands prior to this date.

The golf course is a seaside links with a small parkland element and occupies land that hugs the banks of the River Bush as it meanders out towards the sea. The current layout has been in existence since 1966, after new lands were acquired from the Macnaghten Estate.

The clubhouse has full bar and catering facilities and as a visitor, you'll be assured a very warm welcome. Although the course can be classed as a 'short walk', don't let the lack of yardage put you off. It's a wonderful testing little course set in an area of outstanding natural beauty, another not be missed.

> ***Did you know?*** The club's second ever captain, appointed in 1899 was a lady, a Miss M Creighton, a unique distinction for a club in those days and perhaps a first in Ireland.

The Course

Bushfoot is a nine-holer with two sets of tees that gives a slight variance on the yardage between the front nine and the back nine. Bushfoot shares the attributes of all the other links courses situated on the Causeway Coast, narrow, undulating fairways, small greens that are often raised and thick, un-forgiving rough that will quickly punish any inaccuracy off the tee.

When these elements are coupled with the exposed nature of the course and the tendency for the wind to blow right in off the sea, it makes Bushfoot quite a test for golfers of all abilities.

> *Did you know?* *The ladies theme at Bushfoot continues, every June, for four days the club hosts the Bushfoot Amateur Ladies Tournament, one of the most popular tournaments of its kind in Ireland.*

Hole number & name	Championship yardage	Par	Stroke Index
1 Barney's Folly	408	4	4
2 Runkerry	162	3	12
3 The Himalayas	304	4	18
4 Huey	352	4	5
5 The Bush	408	4	2
6 The Causeway	489	5	8
7 Tram lines	171	3	10
8 Cow's Grave	325	4	17
9 Strawbridge	337	4	14
Out	2956		
10 Barney's Folly	440	4	1
11 Runkerry	135	3	16
12 The Himalayas	348	4	13
13 Huey	352	4	6
14 The Bush	408	4	3
15 The Causeway	498	5	9
16 Tram Lines	191	3	7
17 Cow's Grave	336	4	15
18 Strawbridge	337	4	11
In	3045		
Out	2956		
Total	6001		

The first hole to look out for is the short par-4 3rd, it has a slight dog leg that follows the curvature of the River Bush as it flows along the edge of the fairway and with its blind approach, is a much tougher hole than it first appears.

The Course (cont)

The 171yrd 7th that takes its name from the old Causeway Tram that used to trundle past the course is another of those memorable par-3's, its slight raised green is ringed with bunkers , over-hit your tee shot and you'll find yourself out of bounds, accuracy is everything on this hole.

Our featured hole is the hardest on the course, the par-4 10th, Barney's Folly. Take a moment to enjoy the spectacular ocean view from the tee with the Giant's Causeway in the distance. It's important that you quickly regain your concentration though, take the advice from pro, David Jones, follow his instructions and be careful not to try and cut in too much.

It's often easy to dismiss a 9-hole course, especially one that lacks yardage, whilst a couple of the par-4's are relatively short at Bushfoot, the lack of distance is compensated by the course's finer points, it's certainly worth a visit.

Did you know? *Darren Clarke is a proud honorary member of Bushfoot Golf Club.*

Advice from the Pro!

Golf Coast Northern Ireland has a chat with Bushfoot Golf Club Professional David Jones.

Name: David Jones

Occupation/ Position: Manager / PGA Professional

Course Summary: Bushfoot Golf Club is the hidden Gem of the North Coast. It is a great test in a fabulous location, and a must play for all golfers.

My 3 tips for a visitor playing Bushfoot for the first time:

1) Do not be fooled by the lack of yardage. The constant sea breezes make Bushfoot a challenge for golfers of all levels. The prevailing wind blows across the course offering little help. My advice in windy conditions is simple: take plenty of club and swing it smoothly.

2) Accuracy with your approach shots is the key to a good score here. With many greens raised or surrounded by bunkers it takes accurate approach shots to successfully negotiate your way around this testing links. Missed greens at Bushfoot can be costly! Literally....it will cost you 50 pence at the bar for landing in the "Captains Charity Bunker" on the 9th & 18th holes.

3) Take a few minutes on the 10th Tee to enjoy the wonderful views overlooking Runkerry Bay. I don't believe there is a better view in all the country. Be sure not to get too distracted as the toughest hole on the course awaits you. Many a player has tried to cut off too much and 'paid the price'. I would advise to keep a little to the right and accept a slightly longer approach to the green.

David Jones

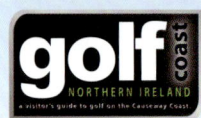

Cushendall Golf Club

A small picturesque 9-holer with spectacular views across the Sea of Moyle to the Mull of Kintyre

"Cushendall Golf Club is a delightful 9-hole course nestling on the shores of Red Bay in the heart of the beautiful Glens of Antrim"
www.golfeurope.com

521 Shore Road
Cushendall
Co. Antrim
BT44 0NG

Tel:
+44 (0) 28 2177 1318

Web:
www.cushendallgolfclub.com

Email:
cushendallgc@btconnect.com

Course Details

Course:
9 holes Par 66 4784 yards

Course Type:
Primarily parkland with some links elements

Intro

The village of Cushendall is situated on the main A2 Coastal Route in the popular Causeway Coast and Glens Area of outstanding natural beauty. Its location at the foot of the River Dall with the table topped Lurigethan Mountain providing the backdrop couldn't be any more dramatic. Three of the nine Glens (Valleys) of Antrim; Glenaan, Glenballyemon and Glencorp converge close to the village.

With the Glens gently rolling down towards the Sea, the scenery here is spectacular. The views from Red Bay, across the Sea of Moyle to the Scottish Isles and the Mull of Kintyre are a sight to behold. The golf course is located on the shore, just outside the village in the shadow of Garron Point, with the River Dall meandering through its holes on its journey to the Sea.

The club was formed in 1937 and although the land in which it occupies is close to the sea, it has more of a parkland nature with some links elements. The course has 9 holes with seven having alternate tees and is made up of three par-3's and six par-4's. Described as an 'easy walking' course, it is relatively flat with several trees and the occasional bump and hollow. Cushendall has a tricky reputation, with the river coming into play on 7 of the 9 holes. This ensures that any wayward shots will almost certainly find a watery grave.

The imposing clubhouse, once known as Legge House was completely rebuilt in 2004 and sits just in front of Cushendall Beach, offering superb views across the bay. Visitors are made very welcome and will be assured what this part of the world is famous for, the legendary 'Glens' hospitality.

Did you know? *The club's badge is a depiction of the 'Children of Lir', a popular Irish legend. Folklore says that King Lir's four children, Fionghuala, Fiachra, Conn and Aodh were turned into swans by their wicked stepmother, Aoife and were banished to spend 300 years in the Sea of Moyle that lies just off the shore of Cushendall.*

The Course

With the River Dall playing such a key role in the majority of the holes at Cushendall, this places a high premium on accuracy off the tee. At 4784yrds and a par-66 it's a short course, but its situation and features will ensure that your round will require a wide variety of shot making.

The opening hole, 'Trostan' at 298yrds looks relatively straight forward at first, but with the river running all the way down the left hand side of the fairway and meandering just 10yrds behind the green, you're advised to keep right. A good tee shot will set up a short iron approach to a green that is well protected with three bunkers and a large overhanging tree to the left.

Did you know? *In 1947, following his Open Victory at Hoylake, Fred Daly made a goodwill visit to Cushendall Golf Club to show off the famous Claret Jug.*

Hole number & name	Championship yardage	Par	Stroke Index
1 Trostan	298	4	11
2 Lurigedan	177	3	7
3 Kilnadore	310	4	3
4 Holm	288	4	9
5 Ailsa Craig	156	3	13
6 Islay	262	4	17
7 Moyle	122	3	15
8 Ossian's Grave	384	4	1
9 Garron	385	4	5
Out	2382		
10 Trostan	294	4	12
11 Lurigedan	177	3	6
12 Kilnadore	331	4	4
13 Holm	305	4	10
14 Ailsa Craig	142	3	14
15 Islay	262	4	18
16 Moyle	122	3	16
17 Ossian's Grave	384	4	2
18 Garron	385	4	8
In	2402		
Out	2382		
Total	4784		

Depending on the conditions, the par-3 2nd requires anything from a medium iron to a fairway wood to help clear the river and end up on the small plateau green 177yrds ahead. Inaccuracy on this hole will be severely punished, anything long will get trapped in the boundary hedge behind the green and if you play short, you'll be stuck in the rough leaving an awkward shot, uphill to the green level. To assure your par, you have two aims, firstly, clear the river and secondly, ensure your shot ends up on top of the plateau.

The Course (cont)

The par-4 8th, Ossian's Grave is rated the hardest hole on the course, your tee shot is straight forward enough, but you must find the centre of the fairway. With the river cutting into the fairway on the right, a good second shot is crucial, if your tee shot is not well placed the trees on the river bank will block your approach to a green that lies in a small hollow.

Our featured hole is the par-4 9th, Garron. The championship tee requires an accurate drive across the river to an elevated fairway. With the green out of sight to the right of the clubhouse and thick rough to the left of the fairway, it's important that your tee shot finds a good position, leaving a straight forward downhill approach to a green that is again, well protected by bunkers and with mature trees to the right.

Compared to the more famous links courses along our coast, Cushendall offers something completely different. With the mountains and Glens providing a dramatic backdrop, it's a delightful little course in a beautiful seaside location, well worth a visit.

> *Did you know?* On the tricky par-3 5th, to save the embarrassment of perhaps having to play a 3 or even a 5 off the tee, the more senior members have been known to lay-up rather than attempting to clear the river from their tee shot. The elevated green lies just ahead of the high river bank, after clearing that, the green is guarded by four well placed bunkers and trees to the left.

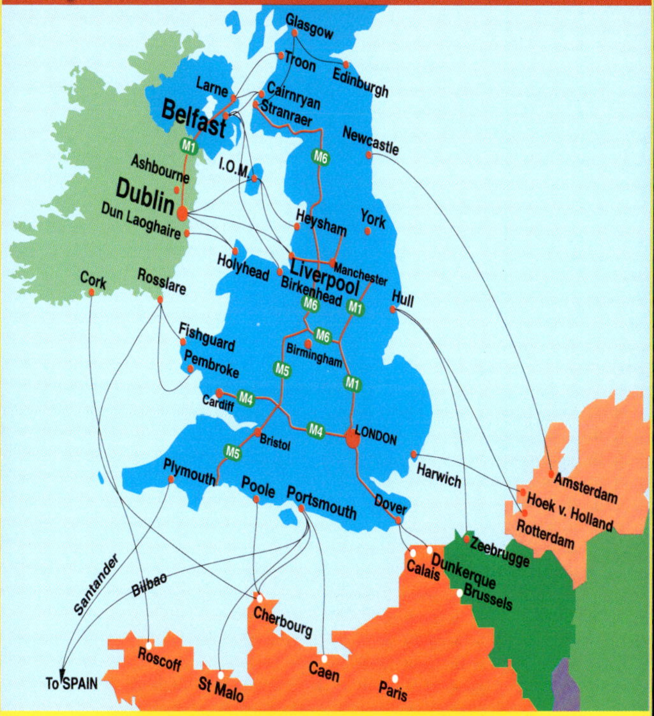

Municipal & other privately run courses.

Ballyreagh Golf Course
1 Glen Road, Portrush, Co. Antrim, BT56 8LX
Tel: +44 (0) 28 7082 2028
Holes: 9 Par: 27 Yardage: 1325

This 9-hole par-3 course is located just outside Portrush on the coastal road that connects the town with Portstewart. The council run facility hugs the coastline with many of the holes offering superb views back across the bay to Portrush. The course is ideal for beginners with many interesting holes. The 5th is played towards the cliff edge and the sea, with the 6th and 8th having to be hit over gaping ravines. There is a well stocked golf shop and the resident professional, Bob Cockcroft has over 35 years experience of golf tuition. There is also a little par-3 pitch and putt, ideal for juniors.

Benone Golf Course
Benone Tourist Complex, 53 Benone Avenue, Limavady, Co. Londonderry, BT49 0LQ
Tel: +44 (0) 28 7775 0555
Holes: 9 Par: 27 Yardage: 1458

This council run course has a reputation as being a tough par-3 nine holer that provides a real test to golfers of all abilities. Set in the shadow of Binevenagh Mountain, the course offers superb views across the surrounding Co. Derry countryside. There are no bunkers but with the rough as unforgiving as it is and with many of the shots played to unsighted greens, the lack of sand is quickly forgotten. Be prepared to lose a few balls! Facilities include a driving range, putting green and a little cafe.

Brown Trout Golf & Country Inn
209 Agivey Road, Aghadowey, Coleraine, Co. Londonderry, BT51 4AD
Tel: +44 (0) 28 7086 8209
Holes: 9 Par: 70 Yardage: 5488

Established in 1973, this 9-hole parkland course forms part of a family run restaurant and inn. Heavily wooded, with each hole lined with mature trees, the River Agivey twists its way around the course and golfers must cross water in 7 out of the 9 holes. The feature hole is the par-3 2nd which crosses the River Agivey twice and has a 170yrd carry, so make sure you choose your club carefully. The course is laid out on clay ground so can get very wet in winter time, but it's perfect for summer play.

Coastal Self Drive Ltd

Coleraine, N.Ireland.

- Van and Minibus Hire -
Choice of Vans, Trucks and 15 Seater Mini-buses

Specialising in Hire to Groups of Golfers
(A Golf Tour Driver/Advisor can be arranged for groups of up to 14 People)

Secure storage trailer and Minibus with tow hitch available for the perfect *'Golfing Tourer'*

tel: +44 (0)28 7035 2791
www.coastalselfdrive.co.uk

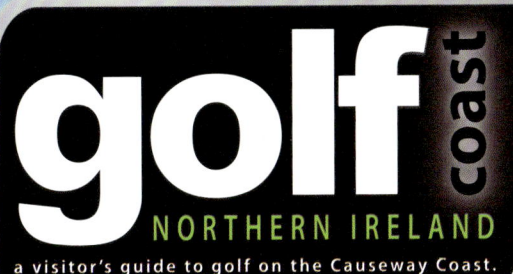

THE NINETEENTH
Tourist Guide

A LOOK AT THE CAUSEWAY COAST'S TOP TOWNS AND ATTRACTIONS.

Portrush

The seaside town of Portrush, home to Royal Portrush Golf Club, proud hosts of the 2012 Irish Open is first and foremost famous for its spectacular location. Situated on a mile long peninsula extending out into the Atlantic Ocean, each side is flanked by a superb, blue flag, award winning beach. The golden sands of the West Strand have a promenade walkway along its entire length with magnificent views across the bay to County Donegal in the Republic of Ireland. The evening sunsets in late spring and early summer turn the sky into a kaleidoscope of red and orange.

> ***Did you know?*** *As well as being famous for its golf, Portrush is renowned for its surfing. There are a couple of specialist surf shops, several surf schools and a pretty active social scene. The Causeway Coast is home to Al Mennie, one of the world's top big wave surfers and the four time Irish national long-board champion, 'Long' John McCurry*

The more exposed East Strand with its towering dunes leads you towards Royal Portrush Golf Club and to the limestone cliffs of the White Rocks. The coastline here has been weatherworn over the centuries into a spectacle of caves and arches with names such as the Giant's Head, the Wishing Arch and the Lion's Paw. The view from here takes in the Skerries, a group of small rocky islets off the shore and on a clear day beyond these to the Scottish Isle of Islay.

> ***Did you know?*** *Barry's Amusements is Northern Ireland's largest theme park and has been a fixture of Portrush since 1925. Still run by the Trufelli family, a trip to Barry's will brighten your day, immerse yourself in the smells of candyfloss and popcorn as you work up the courage to ride the thrilling 'Big Dipper'.*

Top 3 Things not to miss

Digital Art by Stephen Duke

Harbour Bar – The famous Harbour Bar is reputed to be one of the oldest pubs in Northern Ireland. Renowned for serving a superb pint of Guinness, the bar has retained all its 'olde-worlde' charm with its original wooden bar and 'back room' where you can relax by the fire if the weather takes a turn for the worse. It's not unknown for there to be an impromptu sing-song, our advice: forget your inhibitions, pretend you know the words and join in!

Music – Portrush has a lively local music scene, the playhouse theatre attracts some of Northern Ireland's biggest names and there is a multitude of bars and public houses, many of which offer live musical entertainment which showcases the best of local talent. Head for Kiwi's, the 'Quays', the 'Springhill' or the 'Atlantic' for musical weekend feasts. Look out for the Black Dots, one of the area's top local bands.

Eats – Portrush has some fantastic restaurants and eateries, many of these are concentrated in the Harbour area, here you can choose from modern, oriental or bistro-style cuisine. Closer into town, the Restaurant at the Ramada Hotel comes highly recommended, Don Giovani's/ Kiwi's serve a mean pizza and for something more casual try the Ocean Cafe. Reserve some space for an ice cream; Morelli's serve decadent sundaes in the Cafe Lido.

> ***Did you know?*** Portrush plays host to the annual Northern Ireland International Airshow. The crescent shaped West Bay is transformed into an aircraft display area for a weekend every September and becomes a superb natural amphitheatre to watch flying displays from around the world.

One last thing...

If you'd like a little memento of your visit, the town's Main Street has many independent stores that sell the usual seaside souvenirs. The White House is Portrush's very own department store and for antiques and curios visit Kennedy & Wolfenden or the Vintage Stop.

Ask Yer Man!

Golf Coast Northern Ireland has a chat with some local characters that you may bump into on your travels.

Name: Willie Gregg
Occupation: Manager/ Host at the Harbour Bar, Portrush

Willie is the 5th generation of the Gregg Family to originate from Portrush, he takes his position as manager of the Harbour Bar very seriously, "Every visitor to the Causeway Coast should be welcomed and embraced" he says, "It's such a coup for Portrush to get the Irish Open, in relative terms it's comparable to London hosting the Olympics". Willie feels privileged that his job allows him to meet people from all over the world, he's an expert in all things Portrush; in fact you could probably describe the Harbour Bar as Portrush's alternative Tourist Information Office! In his spare time Willie enjoys a spot of fishing and runs his own charity, Willie's Orphan Fund that looks after children in Thailand who were orphaned as a result of the 2004 Tsunami. His fund-raising activities are tireless as he needs to raise a minimum of £2000 per month just to keep the charity afloat. Learn more about Willie's Orphan Fund at **www.williesorphanfund.com**

As a resident of Northern Ireland's Golf Coast, what makes you particularly proud to be able to say that you come from the area?
Our golfing heroes, Darren (Clarke) and Graeme (McDowell) and not forgetting the Daly family are fantastic ambassadors for the North Coast; it makes me very proud that they have brought such success to our little corner of Northern Ireland.

Describe your perfect weekend on the Causeway Coast?
When not working there's nothing better than a drive around the Coast, my favourite stretch is between Magilligan Point and Ballintoy. Every Sunday I bring my Mum, Joan to the Ramore Wine Bar for dinner, then over to Portstewart to have an ice cream in Morelli's. It's the simple things that are the best!

Suggest three essential activities that a visiting golfer should experience during their stay on the Causeway Coast?

1) I have to be biased and say, the Harbour Bar, come along and experience the unique atmosphere, enjoy a pint of Guinness, perhaps have a bite to eat in the new Harbour Bistro and then back to the bar to enjoy a wee drop of 12 year old Bushmills Malt.

2) The Causeway Coastal Route is a must-see. It's a superb driving road and around every corner there's a new spectacular view to enjoy.

3) The scenery at the White Rocks and Dunluce Castle is so dramatic and rugged, for me there's nowhere like it in the world.

Jingles Gift Shop - 15 Main Street, Portrush. Tel: (028) 7082 2874

Jingles and Jaspers Gift shops are located at the heart of Northern Ireland's favourite seaside resort meeting all your gift needs.

We stock cards and gifts for all occasions, whether it be a thank you gift or a gift for someone special. We specialise in personalised and named gifts and have the largest variety any where. Stocking irish souvenirs at an affordable price. We pride our self on a customer friendly approach and will be more than happy to help with your gift selection. We stock many major brands.

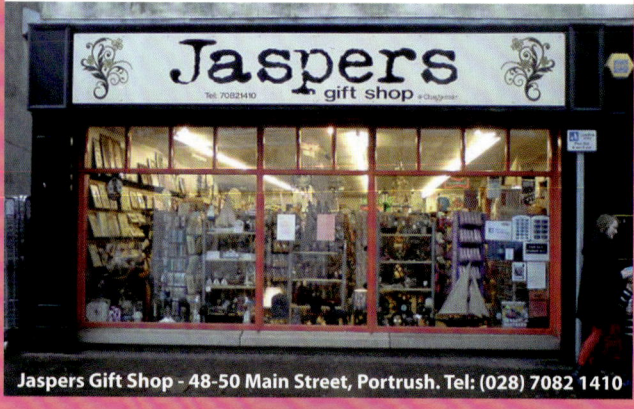

Jaspers Gift Shop - 48-50 Main Street, Portrush. Tel: (028) 7082 1410

www.facebook.com/jinglesportrush

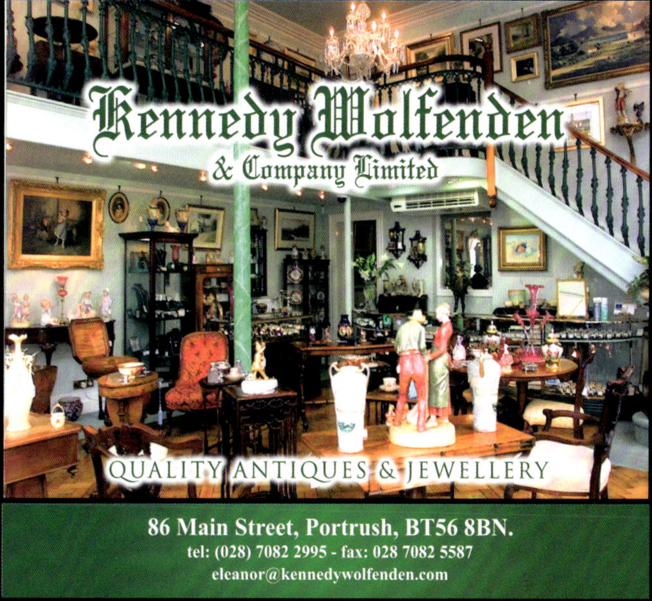

Kennedy Wolfenden & Company Limited

QUALITY ANTIQUES & JEWELLERY

86 Main Street, Portrush, BT56 8BN.
tel: (028) 7082 2995 - fax: 028 7082 5587
eleanor@kennedywolfenden.com

The Vintage STOP

we stock...
Vintage Furniture, Collectables, Clothing,
Jewellery, Accessories & Unique Gifts!

Contact us!
tel: 077 43571129
thevintageshop6365@yahoo.co.uk

JOIN US!

The Vintage Stop,
63-65 Main Street Portrush, BT56 8BN

Portstewart

Portstewart is a small seaside resort that comes alive during the summer months. With its idyllic surroundings, this is the place to be if you want good food, a perfectly chilled Guinness and some banter with the friendly locals. Well equipped with 4 hotels and numerous B&B's you won't be short for a place to stay.

Portstewart is made up of one main street, known as The Promenade with the usual touristy shops, art galleries, an abundance of Ice Cream parlours (more on that later!), bakeries, eateries and bars all along one side, with the stunning Atlantic ocean on the other. From the Promenade you can enjoy spectacular views of Castlerock, Mussenden Temple and the rolling hills of Donegal. If getting away from the hustle and bustle is more your thing, take a stroll along the lower Promenade and watch the amazing sunsets which set the sky on fire.

Top 3 things not to miss ...

Portstewart Strand, a two- mile stretch of golden sand leading right up to the River Bann Estuary. Perfect for an early morning stroll and runs adjacent to the Portstewart Golf Course. You'll find locals enjoying the surf or walking the coastal path which winds all the way back to the Promenade. Stop at the bakery on your way back into the town 'for a wee bun' and you'll be a local before you know it.

Ice Cream! - Home to the one and only Morelli's of Portstewart. With over 100 years of experience behind this Italian ice-cream-making family, a trip to Portstewart is not complete without stopping here to try a famous ice cream sundae while watching the world pass by. Morelli's were recently awarded the accolade of having the UK & Ireland's best Vanilla ice cream in 2012/13.

> ***Did you know?*** *The North Antrim Coast Path that forms part of the Ulster Way, starts at Portstewart Strand and continues for 40 miles along the coast to Murlough Bay.*

Digital Art by Stephen Duke

Fish and Chips! - So you've licked every last bit of your ice cream and drained the last drop of Guinness from your pint glass, the very last thing you can't go home without trying is some Fish and Chips. Don't forget to add plenty of salt and vinegar and tuck in while enjoying the view from the Promenade.

> ***Did you know?*** Morelli's beat the World Record for the longest chain of people licking ice cream in 2011 as part of their 'Cento Anno' anniversary celebrations.

One last thing......

Come visit Portstewart in May, where you will witness The International North West 200 – one of the fastest motorbike road races in the World with speeds exceeding 200mph, bikers (and fans) from around the world gather here for the week-long festival every May to take part in and watch Ireland's largest sporting event. Anyone who loves this sport needs to be part this event at least once in their life. Get caught up in the fast paced, electrifying atmosphere and you'll return year after year!

Did you know?

The view from the Promenade in Portstewart was the inspiration for the Jimmy Kennedy classic song, Red Sails in the Sunset, made famous by Nat King Cole in the early 50's.

ncpm
northcoastpropertymanagement

student | summer | long term | management

Planning a golfing holiday on the Causeway Coast or a trip to the Irish Open? Check out our extensive range of properties available for holiday lets!

+44 (0)28 7083 1950

www.northcoastpropertymanagement.co.uk

Life's too short for bad ice cream..... *thank goodness for* Morelli's to Go!

* Homemade whipped ice cream The largest selection of Morelli's award winning ice cream
* Proper Coffee using freshly ground Bellagio beans
* Sweeties from Aunt Sandra's Candy Factory
* Decadent sundaes and the best milkshakes ever!

ALL TO GO!!

MORELLI'S to GO!
is at 57 The Promenade, Portstewart.

Kiwi's

Kiwi's invites you to come and enjoy some fine New Zealand hospitality on the Causeway Coast. Enjoy a meal from our extensive menu and while you're here, try one of our many NZ Beers or wines, found nowhere else in Ireland.

9-13 Causeway Street
Portrush
tel: 07900 660965

Don Giovanni's

Italian Bistro

- Fully Licensed Italian Restaurant
- Open for lunch till late, 7 days a week
- Large parties and bookings welcome

- Pizza
- Steak
- Pasta
- Fish

(Ask about our 3 course menu for just £10!)

Telephone: 02870825516
Email: dongiovannisportrush@gmail.com
Website: www.dongiovannisportrush.co.uk

Located on Causeway Street, Portrush
Walking distance from Royal Portrush Golf Club

Coleraine

Digital Art by Stephen Duke

Often referred to as the "capital" of the Causeway Coast, the 17th century plantation town of Coleraine is the municipal and administrative centre for the borough of the same name and an ideal base for anyone visiting Northern Ireland's Golf Coast. Picturesque with award winning floral displays and historic architecture, Coleraine or Cúil Raithin in Irish (meaning nook of the ferns) is situated on the banks of the River Bann and has its own university, marina, theatre, leisure centre, parks and pedestrianised shopping area.

One of the most affluent areas in Northern Ireland, Coleraine has a relatively small population of around 25,000 people but has the feel of a small city (it is currently seeking city status) with impressive road and rail links to the Province's capital city, airports, docks and coastal attractions.

> ***Did you know?*** St Patrick's Church of Ireland, located in the main shopping district of the town is built on the site of an early Christian church founded by St Patrick in the 5th century. The site has been used continuously for worship since medieval times and is now home to a neo-gothic 17th century church complete with gargoyles on the bell tower.

> ***Did you know?*** If you enjoy a slice of cheese in your hamburger, it is more than likely that it originated in Coleraine. The Dairy Produce Packers factory in the town is one of Europe's largest manufacturers of processed cheese slices. One popular chain buys over half a billion slices per year!

> ***Did you know?*** It is believed that Mount Sandel Fort to the east of the town is the site of the first known human settlement in Ireland. In the 1970's, wooden houses dating from around 7000 BC were uncovered by archaeologist, Peter Woodman from University College Cork.

photography by Stephen Duke

Top *3* Things not to miss

Shopping – Unlike the neighbouring seaside towns of Portrush and Portstewart with their bustling clubs and bars, Coleraine is not known for its night life. Instead it relies on its reputation as a commercial centre offering a wealth of independent and multi-national stores for those in need of retail therapy during their stay. The town centre is vehicle free and based around the shopping areas of Railway Road, Church Street, The Diamond with its sandstone town hall and a host of picturesque little side streets.

The Outdoors – The scenic Valley of the River Bann with its network of popular woodland walks, parks and water sport facilities make this an ideal location for those who love the outdoors. The self-guided walking heritage trail known as 'Around the Ramparts' provides visitors with an opportunity to see historical sites such as Mountsandel Fort, the forest walk goes from the high point at the fort to the banks of the River Bann and passes close to the weir at the Cutts.

Indoors – The town offers a stimulating range of indoor leisure activities. Its council run leisure centre provides state-of-the-art facilities for a wide range of sporting activities, including a well equipped fitness studio and a large swimming pool. The Jet Centre complex has a multi-screen cinema and ten-pin bowling and the Riverside Theatre on the university campus attracts top international performers from across the whole spectrum of the arts.

One last thing...
The train ride from Coleraine to Londonderry, passing through Castlerock is considered to be one of the World's Most Scenic Railway Journeys. Passing over the River Bann, the sea is seldom out of view, with the Mussenden Temple providing the romantic backdrop.

*For more information on Coleraine visit **www.northcoastni.com***

We plan to make the 2013/14 issue of Golf Coast Northern Ireland even better than this one, if you would like to advertise next year or have any suggestions for features please get in touch. We also plan to include a detailed accommodation listing. Look out for our downloadable ebook version too!

Golf Coast Northern Ireland is produced by:
Vanity Publications
Unit 27 Sperrin Business Park
Ballycastle Road
Coleraine
Northern Ireland
A **morelli** company

www.vanity-publications.com
E: info@vanity-publications.com
T: +44 (0) 28 7034 3283
Follow Golf Coast Northern Ireland on twitter @GolfCoastNI

Endearing your brand to consumers...
through prestigious and beautifully presented publications.

---

fully licensed restaurant

THE WATER MARGIN
fine oriental cuisine

The Boat House, Hanover Place, Coleraine, BT52 1EB.
tel: (028) 7034 2222
www.watermargincoleraine.co.uk

Great Food & Wonderful Hospitality

3 course Tea Time Treat Menu
from £10.50 per person

4 course Sunday Carvery
from £16.00 per person

* 3 Star Hotel

* 56 Guest Bedrooms

* Romanoff's Restaurant

* Elliot's Bistro

* Treatment Room

* Conference & Banqueting Facilities

For more information on accommodation and dining visit:

www.thelodgehotel.com

The Lodge Hotel,
Lodge Road, Coleraine,
BT52 1NF.

Tel: +44 (0) 2870 344848

facebook.com/TheLodgeHotel

Ramada Portrush an award winning hotel situated in the centre of town overlooking the Atlantic Ocean on the Causeway Coastal Route

PORTRUSH HOME OF THE CHAMPIONS

Royal Portrush | 2 minutes drive to 1st tee
Portstewart | 10 minutes drive to 1st tee
Castlerock | 30 minutes drive to 1st tee

Counties Restaurant & Cafe Bar, popular with locals and golfers

info@ramadaportrush.com
Tel: +44 (0)28 70826100
www.ramadaportrush.com

Overall Guest Satisfaction Winner 2011
Ramada Portrush

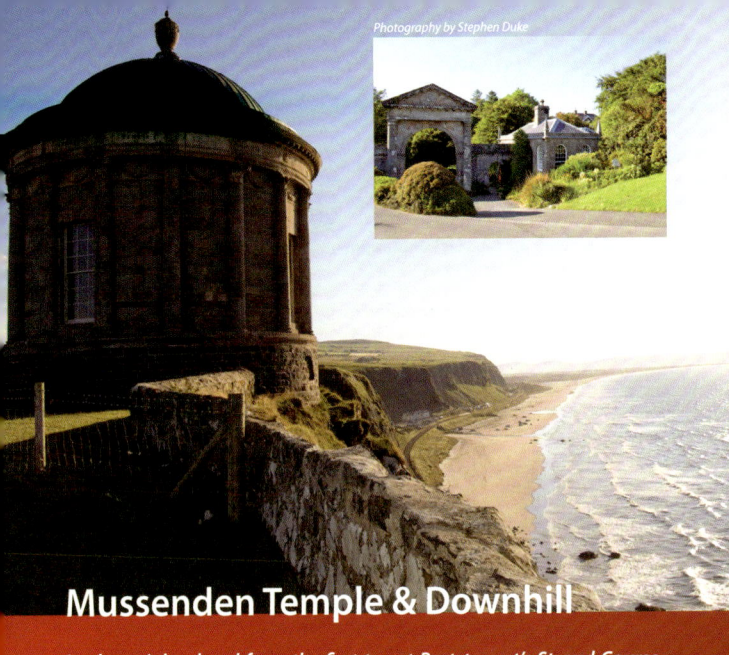

Photography by Stephen Duke

Mussenden Temple & Downhill

Look straight ahead from the first tee at Portstewart's Strand Course and in the distance, right on the cliff edge cuts the imposing figure of Mussenden Temple. The temple, located close to Castlerock is an architectural folly and was built by Frederick Augustus Hervey, Bishop of Derry and Earl of Bristol in 1785 as a summer library. The design was inspired by the Temple of Vesta at Tivoli and is named in honour of his cousin, Frideswide Mussenden.

The views from the temple are spectacular, stretching out over Castlerock, Portstewart, and Portrush with Fairhead in the distance. This is probably one of the most photographed spots in Northern Ireland. The ruins of Downhill House, the once majestic residence of Hervey sit alongside the Temple and even in their current state still manage to have an imposing and majestic air. The history here spans over centuries and includes a devastating housefire and an RAF base during the Second World War.

> ***Did you know?*** *It was once possible to drive a horse and carriage around the temple, but the ravages of the Atlantic and the wild Northern Ireland weather have brought it closer to the cliff edge over the years.*

What not to miss...

For those of you who have not put enough miles on the golf course, the walk through Downhill Demesne is a relaxing way to pass an afternoon. Two miles winding through the beautiful gardens of Bishop's Gate, the peaceful Black Glen, Downhill ruins and the Temple. Watch out for the sheep who take up residence in the winter months however!

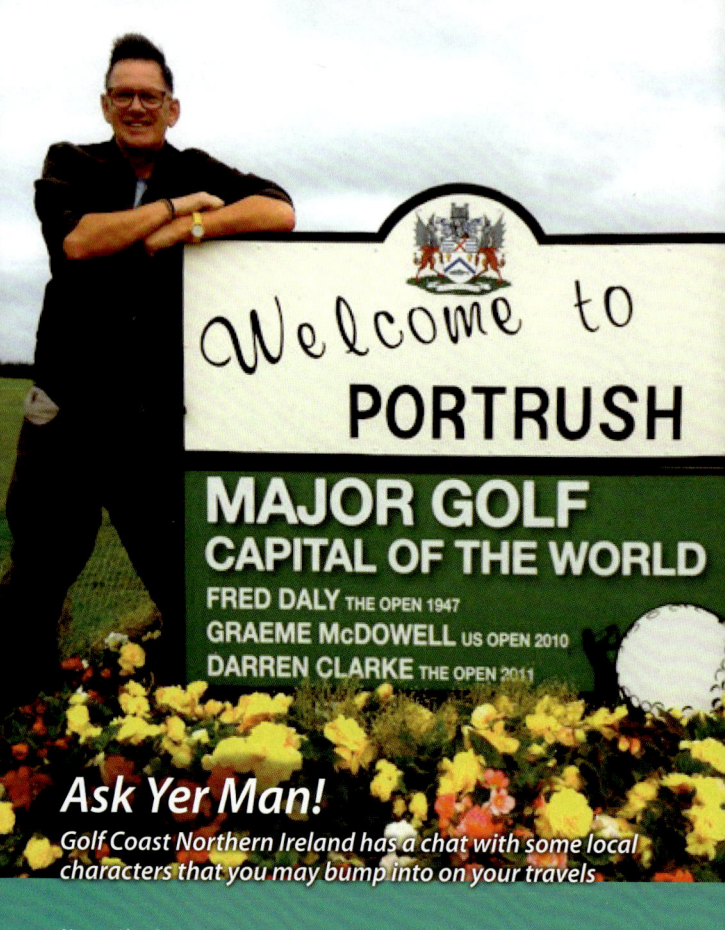

Ask Yer Man!
Golf Coast Northern Ireland has a chat with some local characters that you may bump into on your travels

Name: Alan Simpson
Occupation: BBC Radio Ulster Presenter

Portrush man, Alan Simpson is one of Northern Ireland's best known radio presenters, covering the popular afternoon slot on BBC Radio Ulster. Born in nearby Ballymoney and growing up in Portrush, Alan is fiercely proud of his home town and the Causeway Coast, an area that he has re-christened as 'The Coast with the Most'.

In his spare time, you'll find him either on his bike or in the sea, except that is between 3pm and 5pm most Saturdays when he'll be watching his beloved Coleraine Football Club. It was Alan's idea to mark the achievements of our local golfers on the world stage by erecting the road signs on the approach roads to Portrush welcoming visitors to the "Major Golf Capital of the World". You can catch Alan live on BBC Radio Ulster 92-95FM every weekday from 3pm – 5pm.

As a resident of Northern Ireland's Golf Coast, what makes you particularly proud to be able to say that you come from the area?

Where do I start? When the crowds converge on our Coast for the Irish Open and the world tunes in to the TV coverage they'll quickly realise why I'm so proud to come from here.

From the rugged coastline which boasts some of the best scenery in Europe, comparable in the world to perhaps only New Zealand's North Island to the unspoilt beauty of our beaches with their blue flags and proper golden sand. Then we have our wonderful attractions, the Giant's Causeway, Dunluce Castle and Mussenden Temple, all steeped in history and each with their own unique story.

Describe your perfect weekend on the Causeway Coast?

It would start with a walk on Portrush's West Strand, then perhaps a coffee and a read of the newspapers. In the afternoon or early evening, if it's calm, I'll hit the sea for a bit of stand up paddle-boarding. Then in the evening, there's nothing better than catching up with friends over dinner in one of the many restaurants located around Portrush Harbour.

Suggest three essential activities that a visiting golfer should experience during their stay on the Causeway Coast?

1) Take to the Sea either with a surf lesson, on a kayak or even a fishing charter, by looking up at the golf courses from the sea, you'll see them in a whole new perspective, making you realise just how beautiful our coastline really is.

2) Go for a walk without your clubs. You'll be able to see all the nooks and crannies of our wonderful coast at your own pace, there'll be no lost balls, no shouts of 'fore' and you might even meet a few local characters along the way.

3) No trip to Portrush is complete without a trip to the institution that is Barry's Amusements; after all, we are all big kids at heart.

Photography by Stephen Duke

Giant's Causeway

Photo by Nick Shalinsky's

The Giant's Causeway is Northern Ireland's most visited tourist attraction and the province's only UNESCO world heritage site. The Causeway is an area of approximately 40,000 massive, mostly hexagonal basalt columns that stick out of the sea. Formed by intense volcanic activity some 60 million years ago, the basalt cooled in three separate layers with the middle layer producing the multi-sided shaped stones that we can see there today. Lying at the foot of the steep basalt cliffs the stones creep out of the sea, almost like stepping stones.

Did you know?
Legend has it that the Causeway was actually built by the Irish Giant, Finn McCool as a walk way to Scotland, so he could go and fight the Scottish Giant, Benandonner. Finn fell asleep before crossing and woke up to find Benandonner appearing on the horizon. Realising that the Scottish Giant was so much bigger than himself he ran to his wife Oonagh, wondering what he should do. Oonagh disguised Finn as a baby and made him curl up in an enormous cradle. Benandonner saw the huge 'child' in the cradle and began to wonder what size his father would be. Benandonner fled in fear back to Scotland, destroying the Causeway as he made his way across.

Situated on the Coast, about three miles from the village of Bushmills, the Causeway has a brand new visitor centre (opening early July 2012). The whole project including improvements to the headland is costing a cool £18.5 million, but it's the visitor centre that will impress the most. The sustainable building is cocooned into the landscape with its grass covered sloping roof offering superb views across the whole site. Inside, visitors will be greeted with the latest multi-media technology describing how the Causeway was formed all those years ago.

Photo by Sean Lucas

Top 3 Things not to miss!

The Coastal Path – A spectacular coastal path that hugs the cliffs for some 11 miles connects the Causeway with Carrick-a-Rede Rope Bridge. It passes through the village of Dunseverick and the stunningly beautiful beach at White Park Bay.

Rock Formations –As well as the large group of hexagonal columns that rise out of the sea, there are many other spectacular rock formations located at the Causeway, with names such as the Chimney stacks, the Giant's Boot, the Honeycomb and the Giant's Harp.

The Causeway School Museum - The school was designed by the famous architect Clough Williams Ellis as a tribute to local landowner Lord Edward MacNaghten. Located next to the Causeway and built in 1915, the school is now a museum, giving a wonderful insight into early 1900's schooling in rural Ireland.

> ***Did you know?*** *The Giant's Causeway has been used as a backdrop for many successful photo shoots and advertising campaigns. Perhaps the most famous, is the cover of Led Zeppelin's 1973 Album, Houses of the Holy. The cover was inspired by Arthur C Clarke's novel, 'Childhood's End' and depicts naked children clambering over the Causeway Stones under a blood red sunset.*

One last thing... The recently renovated Causeway Hotel, adjacent to the visitor centre is an idyllic spot to enjoy some afternoon tea.

Royal Court Hotel
★ ★ ★

Occupying one of the best positions on Northern Ireland's most spectacular coastline, the Royal Court offers *unrivalled views over the world famous Dunluce links of the Royal Portrush Golf Club* and also one of the best stretches of beach anywhere on the island.

With 18 well appointed bedrooms and serving freshly prepared food in the hotel restaurant and Grill Room each day, the hotel is an ideal base from which to explore the many superb golf courses in the surrounding area.

JOIN US!

The Royal Court Hotel, Portrush, BT56 8NF
Tel: 028 7082 2236   Email: info@royalcourthotel.co.uk
www.royalcourthotel.co.uk

The Eglinton Hotel

IRISH OPEN ACCOMMODATION SPECIAL

5 Days Bed & Breakfast	£200p.p.s
4 Days Bed & Breakfast	£190p.p.s
3 Days Bed & Breakfast	£180p.p.s

Food served daily from 12.00pm midday.

tel: (028) 7082 2371
Email: reservations@eglintonhotel.com

49 Eglinton Street, Portrush Co.Antrim, BT56 8DZ

Dunluce Castle

Digital Art by Stephen Duke

Dramatically perched, high on a cliff top just outside Portrush is the very distinctive ruin of Dunluce Castle – a must see landmark for anyone visiting the Causeway Coast. Currently undergoing preservation work, the late medieval castle is second only to the Giant's Causeway itself when it comes to popularity, evoking as it does images of princely battles and besieging pirates. Although it never actually housed a prince or princess, the castle does have its own exciting history dating back to the original fortification built in the 13th century by Richard Óg de Burgh, 2nd Earl of Ulster.

Most of the current ruin, however, is 16th century when early records show it was occupied by the MacQuillan family. In 1584 it fell to the famous battle hardy MacDonnell clan who ruled this north eastern corner of Ireland in the 16th century. In 1588, Sorley Boy MacDonnell used his helping of the treasures from the Spanish Armada ship the Girona, wrecked off the Giant's Causeway, to refurbish the castle. After many sieges and battles the castle was finally abandoned by the MacDonnells in the late 1690's.

Did you know? The buildings that currently occupy the rock are almost all from the 16th and 17th centuries, however a 2011 archaeological dig to the west of the castle uncovered remains of a long-deserted town whose ruined church stands in the graveyard south of the castle, separated by the coast road.

What not to miss...

After been handed over to the Northern Ireland Government by the 7th Earl of Antrim in 1928, Dunluce Castle has become one of the most iconic monuments and most popular tourist attractions in the whole of the province. The castle is open all year round and guided tours can be booked in advance. When closed, you can still walk down a long series of steps, past the wishing well and the mermaid's cave, to the stone arch with views out towards the Skerries and the Donegal headlands.

Did you know? During a violent storm in 1639, when the second Earl and Countess of Antrim were waiting for dinner, part of the building including the kitchens collapsed and fell into the sea with the loss of seven of the couple's kitchen staff.

Bushmills

No visit to the Causeway Coast is complete without sampling a tipple of our most famous export. Bushmills is the location for the world's oldest licensed distillery and the whiskey that takes the name of the village in which it's produced has been distilled (legally) here since 1608 when Sir Thomas Phillips received his special license from King James I.

Did you know? Apart from the special aged single Malt whiskeys, Bushmills is produced in two main varieties, the white labelled, triple distilled, Bushmills Original Blend, that is made using Irish grain whiskey and the more distinctly flavoured Black Bush with its high malt content and distinctive black labelling.

Although probably best known for the distillery and its famous whiskey, the village of Bushmills is also the gateway to the nearby Giant's Causeway. In the summer months, a narrow gauge steam railway completes the 2 mile journey from the village to the Causeway. The village itself has its fair share of pubs, eateries, curiosity and gift shops.

> ***Did you know?*** *Bushmills Distillery had its very own steamship, the S.S. Bushmills and in 1890 it set sail from Portrush, on its maiden voyage to deliver Bushmills whiskey to America, calling at New York and Philadelphia before heading on to Asia. When prohibition ended in 1933, the biggest shipment of Irish whiskey ever, left our shores set for Chicago.*

Top 3 Things not to miss

Portballintrae – If approaching Bushmills along the coast from Portrush, take a short detour into the quaint little fishing village of Portballintrae. Its cove shaped bay and sheltered harbour offer some spectacular views across to Scotland's westerly Isles. Take the two mile Cliff top walk to the Giant's Causeway and on your return, enjoy a coffee or something stronger from the renowned Bayview Hotel.

The Bushmills Distillery – The famous distillery tour is one of the most popular visitor attractions on the Causeway Coast. An experienced guide will take you through the whole journey from grain to glass, unlocking the secrets of 400 years of distilling Ireland's most famous whiskey. The tour ends with a wee 'nip' of your chosen blend. For the whiskey aficionados among you, try and get yourself noticed, you may just be lucky enough to get chosen to take part in a more intense tasting session!

The Bushmills Inn – Perhaps almost as famous as the Distillery itself is the Bushmills Inn. With the stables and original coaching inn dating back to 1608, this cosy and charming hotel is steeped in history and tradition. Open fires and a pint of the black stuff is surely a great way to end the day – especially if you have spent the best part of it getting weather beaten out on the course.

> ***Did you know?*** *As well as one of its tributaries providing the water that goes into making Bushmills Whiskey, the River Bush that flows through the village is one of the most famous salmon fishing rivers in Ireland.*

One last thing... If you enjoyed your tipple of Bushmills that much, why not take home a bottle of 1608, a special 400 year anniversary blend, containing 95% malt and 5% grain whiskey made with 30% crystal malt for exceptional smoothness and winner of the Best Irish Blended Whiskey (no age statement) at the 2012 World Whiskies Awards.

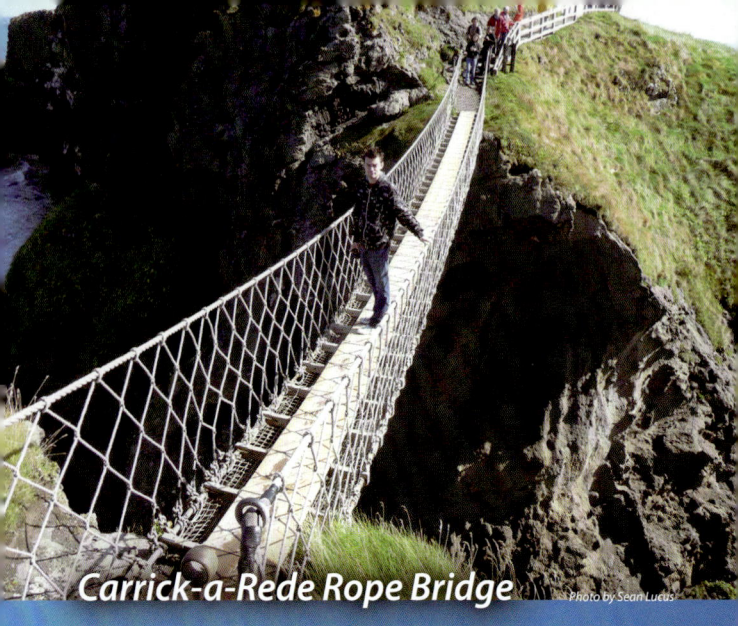

Carrick-a-Rede Rope Bridge
Photo by Sean Lucas

Carrick-a-Rede Rope Bridge is one of the Causeway Coast's most photographed attractions. The 20 metre long rope suspension bridge connects the mainland with the tiny Carrick Island. The bridge was traditionally used by salmon fishermen to tend their nets and it is believed that a rope bridge has existed here for over 350 years. Salmon returning to spawn in the Rivers Bann and Bush once passed this area in their abundance, but with stocks dwindling, salmon fishing here has long since ceased.

Upon arrival at Larrybane Car Park, you'll follow a short coastal footpath along the cliff that leads down to the Rope Bridge. There'll be plenty of opportunities to stop and savour the uninterrupted views across to Rathlin Island and if it's a clear day, beyond Rathlin to Scotland's Westerly Isles. Soaring almost 30 metres above the rocks, the walk across is certainly not for the feint hearted. If you do pluck up the courage to walk across, you won't regret it, the experience will stay you forever.

Did you know? Once you cross the bridge to Carrick Island, there's no 'easy option', you've got to come back the same way. It could be worse though, the bridge used to consist of a single rope hand rail with large gaps between the slats, but this has since been replaced by a more robust, two railed version.

What not to miss...
On the walk down to the bridge stop and look to your left, the Larrybane headland once stretched out to Sheep Island (visible just off the shore) and had a promontory fort dating back to 800AD. Beneath here, there are large caves which once served as a home to boat builders and offered a safe shelter from the fierce winter storms. With sea birds such as guillemots and kittywakes breeding on the islands off the shore, the area has been designated of special scientific interest.

Bayview HOTEL
PORTBALLINTRAE

The Bayview is a family owned hotel located in one of Ireland's most stunning natural settings. Overlooking the ever changing Atlantic Ocean in the picturesque harbour village of Portballintrae, we are conveniently situated one mile from Bushmills on the famous North Antrim Coastal Route.

Only 5 minutes from the famous Royal Portrush Golf Club, home to our Champions Darren Clarke and Graeme McDowell. You may just run into one of our Champions at the Porthole Bar & Restaurant where sumptuous cuisine and excellent weekend entertainment awaits you.

* **25 modern bedrooms designed with your total comfort in mind** *
* **Ask about our new adventure sea safari trips** *
* **Free wifi** *

Bayview Hotel, Bayhead Rd, Portballintrae, Co. Antrim, N. Ireland.
Call us on: +44 (0)28 2073 4100   Email: info@bayviewhotelni.com
Find us on facebook   Follow on twitter @BayviewHotelni
www.bayviewhotelni.com

THE GALLERY
peter nash photography

**20 Main Street
PORTRUSH
BT56 8BL**

'fine art images of the causeway coast'

Tel: 028 7082 5400
Mob: 07876137075

www.giantscausewaygallery.com
www.peternashphotography.com
email: peter@peternashphotography.co.uk

IRISH OPEN
Royal Portrush 2012 County Antrim

YOU THINK IT... & WE PRINT IT!

For all your personalised needs..golf and beyond!

www.tshirtworldportrush.com
3 Eglinton Street, Portrush 02870 823289
Beside Morelli's

OCEAN CAFE

DELICIOUS HOMEMADE FOOD, SERVED WITH A SMILE....

Daily Specials
All Day Breakfast - Homemade Lunches
plus all your favourites and a great kids menu!

Homemade scones, Pastries & Desserts also available to pre-order for collection.

**Contact Marcella: 075 4600 9536
Ocean Cafe, 5 Eglinton Street, Portrush.** (beside Methodist Church)

Causeway Coastal Route

Forget Route 66, The Pacific Coast Highway or Italy's Amalfi Coast, one of the World's greatest road journeys is right here in Northern Ireland. The Causeway Coastal Route takes you along the Antrim Coast and through the celebrated nine Glens of Antrim. Every twist and turn in the road uncovers new sights, over bridges, under arches, through bizarre rock formations and past secluded bays with some of Ireland's finest sandy beaches.

The Causeway Coastal Route is a journey of exploration, where your imagination will be captivated by the breathtaking scenery, dramatic vistas and the rolling green hills and glens. You'll pass some of Ireland most celebrated historic sites, many of which are steeped in local myth and legend.

Did you know? *The modern Coastal Route can be followed from Belfast Lough right through to Lough Foyle in Londonderry but the original Antrim Coast Road section runs for approximately 25 miles from the Black Arch near Larne to the Red Arch near Cushendall.*

What not to miss...

As the Causeway Coastal Route winds its way through the North Coast it takes in some of our most famous tourist attractions including The Giants Causeway, Carrick-a-Rede Rope Bridge and Bushmills Distillery. Other attractions on the Route include:

* *Carrickfergus Castle* – A Norman Castle that dates back to 1177 and one of the best preserved medieval sites in the British Isles.

* *The historic Walled City of Derry,* the United Kingdom's City of Culture for 2013.

Did you know? The original Antrim Coast Road was opened in 1842 and was designed by the civil engineer, William Bald. It was built to improve trading links for the inhabitants of the Antrim Coast and Glens. Before its creation it was easier for them to cross the sea to Scotland to trade goods rather than travel to the nearest town.

Ballycastle

The small seaside town of Ballycastle is located on the north easterly tip of County Antrim and is a perfect central location for those wishing to explore the Causeway Coast and Glens area of outstanding natural beauty. Fairhead to the east of the town is Ballycastle's most prominent landmark, a dramatic cliff that rises almost 200 metres from the sea. The town lies in the shadow of Knocklayde Mountain and is located on the edge of two of the famous Glens of Antrim, Glenshesk and Glentaisie.

> **Did you know?** *Every year on the last Monday and Tuesday in August, Ballycastle plays host to the 'Auld Lammas Fair', Ireland's oldest traditional fair. Thousands of visitors descend on the town to enjoy the carnival atmosphere. Stalls line the streets selling everything from livestock to souvenirs. Traditional delicacies eaten at the fair include 'Yellow Man', a hard honeycomb style sticky toffee and 'Dulse', a type of dried edible seaweed.*

Ballycastle's Main Street has its fair share of shops, bars and restaurants and it leads you towards the seafront with its well appointed harbour and marina, a popular base for leisure craft and fishing trips. It also provides the ferry link to Rathlin, the large island visible just off the shore.

Another passenger service run by Kintyre Express connects Ballycastle with Campbelltown on Scotland's Kintyre peninsula. They also offer private charters, quite handy if you fancy squeezing in a round of golf at Turnberry in Scotland!

Top 3 Things not to miss!

Rathlin Island – Rathlin is Ireland's most northerly inhabited island and is located approximately 6 miles off the shore of Ballycastle. A ferry service and many smaller craft link the island to the mainland. The services land at Church Bay where there is a pub, a shop and the Manor House guesthouse and restaurant. Measuring 4 miles from east to west, Rathlin is a wonderful location for coastal walks and is renowned for its superb scenery and wildlife.

Ballintoy – The village of Ballintoy with its sheltered little harbour is one of the most scenic locations along the Causeway Coast. Situated approximately 5 miles west of Ballycastle, along the main coastal route, the village with its distinctive little white washed church has remained unspoilt by development and has recently been used as a filming location for the Blockbuster US TV series, 'Game of Thrones'.

Kinbane Castle –The ruins of the two-storey Kinbane (meaning White Head) Castle are located on a limestone headland close to the town-land of Cregganboy, approximately 3 miles west of Ballycastle on the Coast road to Ballintoy. The castle was built in 1547 by Colla MacDonnell, brother of Sorley Boy MacDonnell and offers spectacular views out towards Rathlin Island.

Did you know? *The Italian inventor of long distance radio transmission, Guglielmo Marconi used the link between Rathlin Island and Ballycastle to test his wireless technology at the end of the 20th Century. The work was carried out by his assistant, George Kemp but Marconi was said to have visited Ballycastle on several occasions in the late 1890's.*

One last thing... The Moyle way, a twenty mile walk that begins in Ballycastle, ending in Glenarriff Forest Park passes through forest, bog, seaside and mountain scenery and offers the perfect snapshot of the diverse attractiveness that abounds in this part of the world.

Photo by Will Bakker

Cushendall and the Glens of Antrim

Cushendall is small village dating back to the Neolithic era and is a superb location to base yourself in, if you wish to visit the world renowned Glens (Valleys) of Antrim. The beach, shoreline and cliff top walks are all within a short distance of the village that is often referred to as the 'Capital of the Glens'. If you're feeling more adventurous, a hike to the top of the mighty Lurigethan Mountain will result in memorable views out to sea, over the surrounding glens and to the small villages below.

Designated as an area of outstanding natural beauty, the Glens of Antrim are a series of steep coastal valleys and hills located within an area of approximately twenty square miles. The Glens stretch inland from the Antrim Plateau to the famous North Antrim Coastline. The scenery is spectacular and diverse, ranging from sandy beaches and vertical cliffs to boglands, forests, waterfalls and quaint little villages. The stunning natural beauty of the area can be explored by joining the Causeway Coastal Route at Larne and heading north, right into the heart of the Glens.

Did you know? The Curfew Tower in the centre of Cushendall village was built in 1809 as a prison for riotous locals. The design was based on the Great Wall of China. The tower is now an arts centre and is owned by Scotsman, Bill Drummond from early 90's band The KLF.